Pacific Passages

Pacific Passages

Travelling the South Seas

by
Hans-Christof Wächter

Translated by Janina Joffe

 ArmchairTraveller

HAUS PUBLISHING
London

First published in Germany as *Pazifische Passagen. Reisen in der Südsee*
by Picus Verlag

Copyright © 1998 Picus Verlag, Wien

English translation copyright © Janina Joffe 2008

This English translation first published in Great Britain in 2008 by
Haus Publishing Ltd, 26 Cadogan Court, Draycott Avenue, London
SW3 3BX

www.hauspublishing.co.uk

The moral rights of the author have been asserted.

A CIP catalogue record for this book is available from the
British Library

ISBN 978-1-905791-56-9

Typeset in Garamond 3 by MacGuru Ltd
Printed and bound in India by International Print-O-Pac Limited
Jacket illustration: Topham Picturepoint

Contents

Pacific Passages

Prologue

The 180th meridian divides the earth between yesterday and today. Or between today and tomorrow – depending on how you look at it. You can experience this on the island of Taveuni in Fiji – with just one step. Here, not far from a little village named Waiyevo, a sign has been posted on the beach that reads: 'This is where each new day begins'. The arrow pointing east says 'Tomorrow' and the arrow pointing west in the opposite direction says 'Yesterday'. This is both correct and incorrect at the same time. Geographically, it is an undeniable fact that the 180th degree of longitude – the international dateline – runs straight through the island. But, in order to spare the Fijians the administrative confusion of handling two different dates in one country, it was agreed during British colonial times, more than 100 years ago, that the new day should take a swing right just north of Fiji, and pass into the open sea. And that is what it has done ever since.

The texts I have compiled here are about the zones, longitudes and latitudes between yesterday, today and tomorrow, to the right and left of the 180th meridian, the archipelagos of the southern Pacific from Vanuatu in the west, to Tahiti in the east. They are the product of many extensive journeys and visits to the region over the years. The author does not claim to really know this world of endless expanses of water, count-less islands and atolls; the longer he has lived there, the less he knows. He is fully aware that his point of view is that of a foreigner, a view from the outside. The more he became integrated into everyday life, and the more he felt accepted, the more he became (painfully) conscious of this very fact. The stranger's perspective and particularly that of the promoter and lover is always subjective and uncritical. This may be a side note, but could also be seen as a warning to the reader not to miss the subtext: the person writing here has fallen under the spell of this oceanic world completely.

Hans-Christof Wächter

Islands Caught Between the Times

Island-hopping on Vanuatu

Mount Yasur – The mountain stinks. Of sulphur and hell. The mountain is rumbling. It is hissing and roaring. There is no question – it will burst any moment now. It will explode, taking with it the ant-like humans who have frivolously dared to approach the edge of the crater. Glowing red shreds of lava are already shooting through the thick yellow smoke like rockets and are pelting down ominously close to me …

Yakel Village – The men on the levelled dancing square that is located under mighty banyan trees high up in which tree houses are nestled, are small, sinewy and muscular. They keep their arms wrapped around their bodies in the drizzling rain. They are naked, apart from the artful arrangements of bast fibres barely covering their private parts ...

Port Vila – Groups of brown-skinned schoolchildren equipped with notepads and pens are walking past models of rockets and photographs of star constellations, moderately interested. The French embassy has set up a display in its exhibition hall entitled 'En route pour l'espace', the history of space travel. Armstrong's historic footprint, Ariane rockets blasting off, communications satellites. Tomorrow the students will have to write an essay about what they have seen ... The day of the earth's creation, the Stone Age and the departure to the stars. The ancient world and the present. Eras mixing in a small space. Three snapshots, three highlights on an island between the times.

Little of this can be felt on Efate, the main, governing

island. Port Vila, the lively mini-metropolis (21,000 inhabitants) of this 14-year-young homely nation feels present and endearingly intimate. It is no place to be shy with strangers. A certain flair for Parisian nonchalance has remained from the days of French-English condominiums, which in those days were mocked as 'the pandemonium'. British strictness is still represented unerringly by the Presbyterian Church.

The little town lies casually snuggled between the green hills, turquoise lagoons and the beach-lined islands of Vila Bay. There is some slightly nostalgic gingerbread architecture, some hesitant postmodernism and in between there is the usual pan-Pacific corrugated iron sheeting. And there are also palm trees, flame trees, casuarinas, fern trees, banyan trees, tulip trees, frangipani, bougainvilleas and hibiscus … An exuberantly blooming splendour dresses this South Sea beauty like Salomon's silk.

We should have rented a four-wheel drive. We are barely 20 kilometres outside of Port Vila and the small car only manages to climb the deeply eroded canyon at the third attempt. Blonde cows are staring at us unimpressed, chewing thoughtfully, from behind the columns of a coconut palm plantation alongside the road. We are driving 138 kilometres around the island, on the only overland road, which although it is not asphalted, really does deserve this definition, even if only in part. We leave early, following the sun from sunrise onward. This means leaving the city and heading east, then north and then west (and what a sunset it is! One might even call it a deluxe edition with gilt edges!), after which we return home late.

On my right I can see the Pacific at its finest, including perfect travel-brochure beaches, grey ageing coral cliffs that look like knights' castles and fairy palaces, snorkelling lagoons you won't find the world over, white frothy surf on the reef and velvet cushiony island off the shore. On my left I can see land: the constant Trade Wind is rippling over the grass savannah which lies before the distant outlines of volcanoes. Spacious plantations enclose quiet coastal villages and the tangles of lianas make the rainforest seem so tightly locked that not even the eyes can penetrate the green, dark thicket.

The island can easily be circled in one day, but to do it quickly would mean missing out on certain parts. For example: a tremendous view all the way to the Shepherd Islands, a walk to a waterfall in the bush, a swimming break in a deserted cove or a chat with the locals in one of the villages. Rushing would be like messing up a date with a beautiful girl and essentially not deserving any better.

The same principle applies for all the archipelagos of the Pacific: they need time to reveal themselves. The *veni-vidi-vici* conqueror will always lose out in these quiet breadths. But if you choose to give in to these different, calm rhythms, the discovery of leisureliness becomes one of the most pleasing souvenirs.

In order to stretch the duration of your circum-navigation, there are two tiny beach resorts about half-way around the island, on the north coast of Efate. They are so idyllically out of place that they may just persuade you to add on a few days of relaxation far removed from the rest of the world.

Everlasting beauty is undisturbed. Ancient magic has, however, long been banished from Efate by the white people, who had their first base here in the New Hebrides. And yet, on Pentecost, only 200 kilometres to the north, magic is still mighty, determines the lives of the islanders and connects these people with the forces of nature in a mysterious way.

Above him the sky stretches as far as all the horizons and below him the palm fronds are rustling in the wind. Tucked in between are the reed roofs of his village, Rangususu, the endless blue of the ocean in the distance – he stands above all of it. Soromone stands on a fragile little platform at the very top of the tower, dressed only in a bark belt in which the tip of a quiver containing his penis is attached. His muscular body is shining and bronzed, covered in coconut oil. This is the one great moment of the year. Everyone is looking up towards him, staring only at him. For just a few moments he, Soromone, is at the centre of the world, in unison with it. He savours this moment. His body becomes a spring of steel, every muscle is tensed. He spreads his arms, looks up to the sky and shouts-cheers-begs his need to jump and the fear of falling into the distance with a high-pitched scream

— his last moment alive or his triumph. He holds on to this moment before slowly crossing his arms on his chest in a ritual gesture and lets himself fall forward in slow motion. A moment of truth on the brink of 30 metres of emptiness.

Right before he would hit the ground, the lianas that are tied around his ankles and fastened to the top of the tower are tautened. Hanging upside down, his body swings to a halt a few centimetres above the loosened earth. A few villagers pick him up, cut him loose and congratulate him. Once again Soromone has completed the annual Pentecost Jump.

This ancient form of bungee jumping has been named the *Naghol* by the islanders. It is a mixture of an archaic ritual, a manly test of courage, a dance festival and a village fun-fair. This is the only place on earth one can witness such a breathtaking game of gravity that can't really be defined in our words. The British have named it 'Land Diving' but in the circus it would probably be announced as a death jump. The *Naghol* has made a tiny remote island famous.

The island was first put on the world map by

Bougainville, a Frenchman circumnavigating the globe. On 22 May 1768 he wrote: 'Because it was Pentecost, we named it the Pentecost Island.' And that was that. (These 'discoverers' were rarely interested in the names that these islands were given hundreds of years earlier by their native inhabitants.) So it was christened Pentecôte or Pentecost. Today it is still far off the beaten track, very unspoilt, wild and friendly, in short: undiscovered by tourists.

Almost, at least. Because once a year, the *Yuropin*, the curious white people with photo and video cameras, come to visit the island. This happens for a few days in April and May when the *Naghol* is celebrated. The chiefs have, however, decided that there can never be more than fifty of them at the same time. The *Naghol* is not to deteriorate into touristy folklore; it is to stay what it has been for many generations: the most important festival in the cycle of a year, a prayer for a rich harvest of yams, a ritual to keep the spirits in check and a proud, self-confident celebration of the *Kastom*, their traditional way of life.

As a result, the traveller does not feel like a paying

voyeur as soon as his feet touch the white sand. He is welcomed, entertained and accepted as a guest. Chief Henrik, the only one who speaks English, does the honours and leads the strangers – there are merely four of us – to the festival grounds. The national slogan has been emblazoned on his t-shirt in *Bislama* and reads: '*Hapi Tumas Long Vanuatu*' which is supposed to mean as much as 'Happy too much in Vanuatu' or just 'Totally happy in Vanuatu' which can only be confirmed by us.

Bislama is the ridiculous toddler-pidgin-English ('*glas blong lukluk big*' = 'glass for looky looky big' = binoculars) that the merchants and missionaries taught the islanders in the 19th century because they assumed their intelligence wouldn't suffice to learn 'proper' English. In the meantime it has developed into an independent language which serves the nation of eighty islands and over 100 idioms as a national language.

Behind the village a tower rises into the sky above a hilltop. At first sight it appears a slapdash patchwork of a structure, that would give any health and safety inspector a heart attack, but on closer examination turns out to be an ingeniously constructed scaffolding with seven storeys, tapering toward the top and anchored with cables made of lianas. It is light and elegant, made of logs, bars and bark straps without a single nail. The strange edifice stands erect like the large sculpture of a Beuys-student above the palm trees in the beaming South Sea skies. Fifteen platforms on different levels facing the hillside announce that we will see fifteen jumps in total.

Slowly the village gathers and we receive another surprise. The same men and women who greeted us on the beach in t-shirts, jeans, shorts and skirts are now wearing grass skirts in just the same matter of fact way, and certainly not to please us tourists. How does this all fit together? They are Catholics but believe the forest is inhabited by the spirits of their forefathers; they are experts at repairing outboard motors but practise sacrificial rituals in which the highlight is the slaughtering of dozens of pigs; they use insecticides to protect themselves from malaria but throw themselves off of towers to guarantee a good harvest.

Their 20th century is the same as ours, and yet their roots reach deep down into another world. They live in between the times and haven't turned schizophrenic in the process.

The first and youngest jumper is only ten years old. When he steps out onto the platform of the lowest tier his face is a fixed mask of grown-up concentration. After all, six metres can be a long way down. His father is standing at the bottom of the slope, demanding confidence with his arms outstretched. The beseeching song of the others becomes louder, the stomping dance more hectic. Until the boy lifts his arms into the air. Abruptly the singing ends and the dancers are still. Now he is in control. The only thing left making a sound is the wind in the palm trees. There he stands, very alone and very small. And then he jumps. He is caught, untied, congratulated and he skips back happily to his family.

Some take longer to overcome themselves and some offer a more acclaimed performance than others, but no one succumbs to fear. Breakdowns do occur, so no one overstrains himself. For this is not a competition against the others, it is purely a fight against oneself. The difference between the second highest and the top level is only two metres, but the last and furthest jump is limited to the master of the tower as the crowning moment. After fourteen previous jumps, even we, the pale, long-nosed foreigners can tell that Soromone displays a masterpiece of body control, concentration, timing and showmanship.

We also take a jump. This time to another island. But which one? Perhaps to Espirito Santo, Vanuatu's largest island, with its famous diving areas which include artificial reefs from the Pacific War, among them a 22,000-tonne troopship. Or should we head for the mysterious Malekula where cannibalism was allegedly still practised in the jungle villages of the *Big Nambas* until the middle of the 20th century? Maybe to Erromango, the 'Island of Martyrs', which had the greatest loss of missionaries at that time? To the crater lakes of Ambae? Or to Ambrym with its smoking volcanoes, to Epi or Aneityum?

The *Dugongs* tip the scales. Franz Schmöllerl, who really ought to know, says: 'On Tanna you can find every opposite to Vanuatu in a nutshell.' The Austrian doctor, author, pilot, shark specialist and dropout has been sailing the waters of the South Seas for fifteen happy years. 'You can see active volcanoes, hot springs, rain forests in their most primordial form, and villages in which the Cargo-Cult is worshiped; there are also wild horses on expansive grass plains, caves full of flying foxes and even a cove with *Dugongs.*'

'*Dugongs?*'

'A couple of sea cows. They are so trusting that the kids swim with them.'

So we are heading for Tanna and hopping 400 kilometres south of Pentecost. We fly through white cotton clouds over lush green hills, black lava cones and surf-surrounded ring atolls across deep blue endless waters.

In order to spare you any disappointment, I will tell you straight away that we did not see the *Dugongs.* The sea was too rough for such an encounter. Either way, it would have been a melancholy rendezvous since only one animal is still living in Port Resolution. His/

her partner was accidentally caught by a fisherman who mistook the creature for a large fish. Be it male or female, the lonely sea cow is living in a historically significant place: James Cook named the large bay in which he anchored in 1774 after his ship. The name of the island also originated from Cook. It is the result of yet another misunderstanding between the discoverers and the involuntarily discovered, who could only attempt communication through pantomime. The Englishman wanted to know the name of the island and pointed to the ground. Chief Paowang responded with the word for 'the ground' and said *'Nuktanna'*. Cook only caught half of the word, the wrong one at that, and consequently the island was named Tanna.

Cook also wrote the first detailed description of the island, its inhabitants and natural phenomena. For instance that of the Yasur volcano: 'which we watched expel tremendous amounts of smoke and fire with a deafening noise that could be heard for miles'. They could not climb the volcano because the islanders forbade it – the mountain being a strict taboo. Cook respected this, but today people are not as exact about this rule. If the foreigners want to go to the volcano, they can do as they please. But only if the right amount of cash is presented to the volcano owner. Currently this title is being fought over by three villages. The Solomonic solution to this problem is that the mountain guides are provided in rotation from one village at a time.

After hours of bumpy driving through the jungle and up the mountain across grey ash heaps in a dead no-mans-land we stand at the edge of the roaring gorge – with absolutely no railings in sight. It may be rationally reassuring to know that there has not been an eruption recorded since Cook's times and well before that, but this doesn't do much to help control a weak stomach and the most primal fear of uncontrollable fire.

There are three vents smouldering, hissing and spitting deep inside the mighty crater. Red lava is swelling out of them while stinking sulphurous steam whirls up and is sucked back in momentarily. There is a sudden moment of menacing silence until fountains of glowing chunks and bizarre lava shreds shoot into the evening sky with a deafening crack. This spectacle repeats itself at regular twelve-minute intervals. The danger of this experience should not be underestimated. A few years ago a Japanese tourist was struck dead by some falling debris. Our previous desire to climb the mountain, soon became an equally strong urge to hear the 'old man' (the translation of *Yasur*) mumbling comfortably at a safe distance.

This can be done in Sulphur Bay, one of the three villages claiming ownership rights over the volcano. Sulphur Bay leaves a depressing impression: bamboo and reed huts are in need of repair; the fences are battered and provide no barrier to the scavenging pigs that have turned the grass quadrangle at the centre of the village into a freshly ploughed field. Even the villagers here seem ragged and sullen. In light of the many tidy villages and friendly inhabitants we have seen so far, this kind of neglect is bewildering. The instability evident here can be explained with one simple fact: Sulphur Bay is a John-Frum-Village.

Seemingly out of nowhere, a new cult was created

on Tanna in the 1930s. Its messiah, the mysterious John Frum, appeared from the sea one day with the promise that the cargo of the white men would be returned in to the islanders in abundance very shortly. Consequently, it was a clear waste of time to keep slaving away to earn money and store up food. When soon after American troops flooded the island during the Pacific War and their camps were stocked to excess with goods, the cargo-cult acquired new momentum and a decidedly pro-American touch. The islanders marvelled at their parades and flag ceremonies and were fascinated by the medical treatments they received in tents that were decorated with red crosses. There was no question that John Frum (John from America) had to be an American. At present, he is said to be living deep in the bottom of Mount Yasur with his 5,000 warriors. It is not long before he will return, to build his empire …

Until then, there will be a ceremonial raising and lowering of the American flag every morning and evening in Sulphur Bay. The locals will also continue to parade in hand-made 'American' uniforms with bamboo rifles and will pray and sing to John Frum in front of a red cross. Only the absolute minimum is done to maintain day-to-day survival. After many decades of waiting, this bizarre religion has lost some of its impetus and its followers flaunt the factious and bitter mien of now-more-than-ever whilst the young state of Vanuatu is rather embarrassed by all of this. Unfortunately the situation is too bleak to be funny. It reduces the blessings of Western civilisation to syphilis and atomic testing – leaving only an absurd feeling behind.

In Yakel, however, the 'Stone Age village' (as it is described in travel brochures) deep in the rain forest, the world still seems to be all right, the way it was hundreds of years ago before the first three-masters appeared on the horizon. It is as if time had stopped here a long long time ago. We are the only ones who seem absurd here, with our umbrellas, brightly-coloured rain jackets, cameras and notepads. Here, people wear the only thing suited to this kind of temperature, namely their skin. 'One can hardly say that they cover their natural bareness' was the euphemism chosen by Captain Cook to discretely describe the facts. Ever since a road was built leading into the village, the great wide world comes into Yakel. The inhabitants of the village accept this calmly.

Senior chief Kauiya, who claims to be 117 years old – and the wrinkles around his eyes deepen as he smiles – allows the white giants to be lead through the widespread village and surrounding gardens and tells stories from his life: When he was working on the construction of a new airport in Port Vila, Prince Philip visited the village ... and so he lets someone bring him the photo album. These are old stories and legends that are told over and over and passed on whilst everyone is huddled closely around the fire in the meeting house and rain beats down onto the roof above. So many stories to tell ...

The Island of Ovalau

A quick trip back in time to the early days of establishing contact

Fiji? Where is that? No idea. But wait, yes: 'Fidshis' is what Germans use as a derogatory term for the Vietnamese. (That is, if the insult doesn't turn into assault as well.) To these people Vietnam is on one hand the Far Eastern country that has been war-torn for decades and on the other hand it is Fiji, the South Sea archipelago of 300 islands. The fact that there are thousands of kilometres of ocean in between doesn't seem to concern such ignorant people. The world can be that small. I wonder if the Vietnamese and the Fijians would get along if they ever encountered each other, particularly if they knew that racist German fools thought they were one and the same people. Or perhaps they would also beat each other to death, being that one country is Buddhist and the other Christian ...

But we shall stick to Fiji, the island state in the South Pacific, located nearly four hours by air northeast of Australia. Fiji is like Mallorca or Tenerife for Australians – its holiday value being identical. You can get away from everyday stress for two or three weeks, go to a foreign country which is inexpensive and friendly, get your fill of sun-sea-and-sand and experience a new lifestyle, but everyone speaks English. If one goes by the dominating accent on some of Fiji's islands one might almost assume they were conveniently anchored in the Great Barrier Reef.

But let's not be unfair: all of the little islands belonging to the Mamanutha Group or those along the Coral Coast of the main island of Viti Levu, which are filled with beach hotels and tropical sea air, are beautiful and most definitely suited for a perfect holiday. But, if you will forgive me for saying this, they are not really Fiji. They could, for instance, just as well be in the Caribbean.

The real Fiji is different and takes place some-where else – for example on the small volcanic island of Ovalau. The town of Levuka was the first capital city of Fiji, in the days when the last independent cannibal king was forced to submit to Queen Victoria in 1874 and place his country under the trusteeship of the British Empire.

It is thus a place filled with history, a woman of the world, who has nonetheless seen better days. Since then, she has become run-down, a little on the bizarre side but ever so charming. When Suva on Viti Levu was named the capital shortly after the Deed of Cession and expanded accordingly, Levuka was forgotten, let herself go and stopped changing her clothes. She is still wearing those same clothes today. She is a small colonial town in the tropics, wearing the frayed crinoline dresses of the 19th century. The tilting framework and flaking paint of the wooden facades and colonnades of Beach Street would provide an ideal set for a western-style showdown, just like one might expect to see Wyatt Earp and Doc Holli-day toasting victory in the bar of the Royal Hotel.

In the past as well as today (for lack of alternatives) the Royal remains the most important building in the square. One hundred and fifty years ago,
it provided lodging for Captain Ahab's colleagues,
the captains of whaling ships. This explains the small
platform with a balustrade on the roof of the hotel:
it is a crow's-nest used to keep a lookout for ships. It
seems that not much of the interior furnishing has
changed since then either. The rooms are separated
from one another by walls made of boards, the beds
are hand-made and the gigantic billiard table is an
antique that, along with the rest of the furnishings
and the staff, needs a preservation order.

In the early 1860s Levuka was a boom town and
the roadstead was a dense forest of masts. Drunken
sailors, adventurers and bankrupts from all parts of
the world moved noisily through the hotels, bars and
other establishments. It was even said that in order
to find the entrance to the port of Levuka, one only
needed to follow the trail of empty rum bottles drifting out of the lagoon with the tide.

In an edition of the *Fiji Times* from those glory days

the following sentence can be read: 'In the past week, we have had enough fights to fill an entire month. And if broken noses, black eyes and narrow escapes from being slit open with a samurai sword still don't make us walk the streets with revolvers at our waists, then our wish for a magistrate who will finally clean up this drunken riffraff has grown even stronger.' Added to that there were occasional desperate attacks by the nearest native tribe, who after living on the island for generations, irritatingly wouldn't accept that the Whites should now control their island. One thing is certain, in those days Levuka was anything but boring.

'Here lies Elise Marie Antonie Krafft. Born in Düren on June 5th 872. Died in Nasova Levu on July 28th 1906. Rest peacefully in foreign soil.' This inscription can be found chiselled into an ornate tombstone in gothic script behind a rusty cast-iron gate in the cemetery on Levuka. Although I am in no hurry to die now, this place strikes me as a good place to be laid to rest. Half-way up the hillside the palm trees are swaying in the Trade Wind, the frangipane is blossoming in a creamy yellow and the rolling grass hills look over the turquoise-blue-jade-green lagoon, the white surf on the reef, deep azure waters all the way to the horizon and above it all the endless sky. I love this place with its predetermined melancholy and natural cheeriness and I always come back to this spot; to have a chat with Mrs Krafft and envy her view.

Who was this young Rhinelander who died so far from home on a notorious dark cannibal island? Was she the wife of a German trade representative or planter? She was certainly a wealthy woman, since the elaborate monument is made of marble. I looked for her. She was only thirty-four years old when she was carried to her grave in this foreign soil. How old might she have been when she left Bremerhaven, Germany and Europe behind to embark on a strenuous four-month journey half way around the world just to land on the beach of Levuka and be embraced by her husband? Did she come gladly, excitedly anticipating this new world? Or was the marriage arranged by her family, like so often in those days, in order to suitably marry-off at least one of several daughters?

A few years later I did find her. Well, a few traces at least. They were very endearing. A copy of the *Cyclopedia of Fiji* from 1907 is kept in the parliament library in Fiji's capital city Suva. This is the 'Who's Who' of the colony. Her entry can be found under 'Levuka – The late Mrs. Krafft' and states that her husband (who does not have an entry of his own!) owned a sawmill at the time of her arrival and was later named Imperial German Consul. And her house in Levuka was so well known for its hospitality that anyone who ever stayed there never forgot it. This was due to Mrs Krafft's kindness and charm. 'With the proverbial jolliness and liveliness of the Rheinlander' she made every guest feel content and comfortable in her home. Her selflessness is also praised, along with the patience she showed in dealing with her long-term illness. Are the everyday stories from someone's life the truly interesting part? By now they are faded and untraceable.

There are a striking number of gravestones with German names in this cemetery for dignitaries. Some of them show the date of arrival on Fiji next to the dates of birth and death engraved into the stone. I soon notice that for the first generation of German immigrants this date is shortly after 1850 and certain connections begin to reveal themselves. These people were political émigrés, fleeing Germany after the 1848 Revolution and the subsequent crackdown on democrats. In short, asylum seekers who were driven all over the world and mostly ended in America. But a few particularly adventurous ones travelled all the way to the islands glorified by the explorers Bougainville, Cook and Forster as paradise on earth.

When the young Mrs Krafft arrived on Levuka from Düren, the city had long become well-mannered. And was starting to go downhill. Marie Antonie will have danced in the ballroom of the town hall, whilst men entertained her with stories from the wild old glory days when during the American Civil War they had made good money in Fiji from cotton and the whale-oil trade was still profitable. Even then the golden colonial days were long past.

The door of the town hall is heavy with age and creaks open slowly. It reveals a wide empty space with the sun drawing tracks of light on the worn floorboards through lattice windows. There is a high concert podium, a few stacked chairs, slim cast iron pillars and the shadows of intricate murals on crumbling plaster. It is the distant fading glory of the European *fin de siècle*. And yet, the meagre, disused assembly room has managed to maintain its aura, in spite of all its shabbiness. It is easy to imagine the festive jostle of a ball with an orchestra smoothly playing a waltz … 'Mrs Krafft, may I have this dance? Is madam already taken?'

One could then eat the sorbet accompanying the midnight fireworks next door on the veranda of the Ovalau Club. Yes, it too has seen better days. Annie Taylor, its English-Tongan-Fijian manager can confirm this, as her family has been running the club for three generations. The members-only sign on the door of the veranda didn't stop us from dropping in for a Fiji bitter and a chat at the bar beneath faded photos of three-masters, dignified-looking bearded gentlemen in cricket whites and the Queen Mother in her younger years.

We are curious to inspect this gallery more closely. Annie notices and has her fun talking to us. 'You are from Germany, right? I can tell. I know what you are looking for. The letter from the Count to my grandfather, right?' Right. She reaches under the table without saying a word and presents us with a dark hand-carved frame. In this frame, under the glass, there is a hand-written letter, graceful script on aged brown paper. So this is it, the famous letter that Count Felix von Luckner should really not have written! It is difficult to decipher, but assures a Mr Thomas Stockwell (in English) that he regrets not having met him. 'My men and I slept in your house and ate a good meal. Now we are fit to continue our pleasure cruise again. The provisions we took have been paid for: 1 turkey 10 shillings, bananas 3 shillings. Yours truly, M. Pemberton.'

The story behind this is as follows: In the classical style of 18th-century buccaneers, the imperial naval officer von Luckner began an almost anachronistic commerce-raiding cruise in his sailing-ship *Seeadler* ('Sea Eagle'). He soon became known and feared across all the oceans. Known for his chivalry, feared for his success rate at sinking ships, he was known as the 'Sea Devil'.

When his ship was thrown against a reef near Tahiti, this warhorse was nowhere near giving up. With a handful of trusted companions he made his way westward in a dinghy, as once Captain Bligh had done after the mutiny on the *Bounty*, to capture a ship and name it *Sea Eagle II*. They made a rest-stop on Mr Stockwell's plantation island, where they arrived half-starved and nearly dying of thirst. The Count wrote his dutiful thank-you letter and the continued on. As it turns out, his aristocratic etiquette did not pay off: 'Mr Pemberton's' English was far too poor for him to be the well-known British travel writer he claimed to be. Moreover, the curvature of his 'S' was clearly from a German hand.

They went to search for him and were successful. On 21 September 1917, not far from Ovalau, on Wakaya, a small police contingent surprised themselves by overwhelming and actually capturing the heavily armed buccaneers. The Fijian provincial gendarmes only succeeded in these efforts because Count von Luckner put up no resistance whatsoever. The reason: the Count was not wearing his uniform, and an imperial officer could not fight in civilian clothing. This is how the 'Sea Devil' himself describes the scenario anyway – but he was well known for his cock-and-bull stories.

Similar stories are also told in these parts and everyone takes them at face value. They fit and belong to the way Levuka still presents itself – as a living reminder of long-gone colonial history. It comes complete with the small ageing temple that is the *oldest* freemasons' lodge in the Pacific (1875), the shining white structure of the *oldest* public school (1879) which is an impressive example of tropical colonial architecture, and the *oldest* warehouse of the venerable Morris-Hedstrom-Company, recently saved from demolition and turned into the charming little Community Centre Museum. There is a reminder of Victorian history that follows you everywhere you go on Levuka, that lively island town on Ovalau that lies between green volcanic mountains and the deep rolling Pacific Ocean.

The Way the World Should Be
Everyday life on Fiji

This time it has to work. My reputation is at stake. I circle around the mushroom-shaped coral with very slow beats of my flippers and come within 3 metres of the school of blue-green parrot fish who are fervently gnawing at the rocks of coral in the soft light of diagonal sunbeams. I can clearly hear the snap-snap of their beaklike mouths and I can see the finely-ground coral chalk crumbling from their gills. (So this is how the South Sea beaches are made!) There are nearly thirty big ones right in front of me.

This time it will work. I couldn't possibly miss them. How beautiful and peaceful they look, floating in the clear water of the reef … I can see it, but at the same time I can't: they are now my prey, sustenance for the village. I carefully place the spear into the wire sling along with the elastic between my left thumb and index finger and pull it back. Exactly the way we cocked our slingshots as boys when we hunted Indians or sparrows.

Pow! I shoot – and miss. Again! Tawake and Mara have to swim to the surface as fast as they can so as not to choke on their laughter underwater. We have been snorkelling around the reef for an hour and both of them already have a ring full of fish tied to their belts. But I just can't seem to figure it out … even though it looks so easy. Patiently, one of them dives to the bottom again to retrieve my wandering spear from the sand. This ancient form of hunting wild fish is called *Gilbertising* here on Fiji. The simple technique originates from the Gilbert Islands up near the Equator. If you have mastered it, it can be very successful. I have not mastered it. This makes it particularly fun. The Fijians love nothing more than some unexpected fun and practical jokes. That is why the twin brothers Tawake and Mara, whom I still can't tell apart after eight weeks as a guest of their family, like to take me fishing. It will always provide them with something to laugh about.

The first time I went hunting with them in these waters, I didn't really feel like laughing at all. In the meantime I am slightly more case-hardened when I hear them speak of eels, stingrays and sharks. But at first! While we were paddling out to the reef Tawake – or was it Mara? – mentioned 'Those are two towers, they grow from nearly 20 metres depth. They belong to a stingray – a big one.'

'What do you mean by "belong"?'

'He lives there. It's his territory.'

Mara adds in passing: 'And an old eel also lives there. It's about as big as I am and as thick as a palm tree trunk. Green and spotted. What a beauty! But completely harmless. I think you just shouldn't get to close to her cave. The same goes for the stingray. Most of the time he just lies in the sand dozing.'

'And sharks?'

'Hardly any. Well, sometimes one comes in

through the passage with the tide and looks around. But they aren't interested in us. Completely harmless. Don't worry, we come out here a lot.'

I'm not worried, because I know that I am with experienced fishermen, even if they are both only eighteen years old. But let's just say that when I slide off the side of the canoe I am *very* attentive.

The two lumpy baroque towers grow out of dusky sand which sinks into a contourless darkness into the passage in the reef wall from where the current emanates. They are encrusted with pillows, chalices and fans made of sulphur yellow, fluorescent blue, crimson and pink sprawling corals. Velvety smooth and rounded or pointed and stiff like spiny bushes, in between squishy bloated sponges, fine rosettes of feathery worms like finest Brussels lace, the soft blue marbled lips of giant mussels, and the dunes cradle fields of countless transparent pale and bubbly anemone tentacles surrounded by swarms of thousands of reef fish in all colours of the rainbow ...

Tawake introduces me to his territory and points down: look, the stingray, careful! I can vaguely make out a large triangular shape almost completely covered in sand. Tawake waves to me, and as we come half way around the larger the rock he points down again: look out, the eel. At first I can only see a dark and overgrown cave. I will certainly remember to avoid the place.

After half an hour of partly successful and partly frustrating fishing – at least now I can find my spear myself, sometimes – Tawake taps me, makes a calming gesture and points into the blue. A shark! A large grey torpedo, elegant, cold, efficiently steering towards us from the reef passage in a slow wide arc. And soon a second and third large body materialise behind him in the dark distance. They slide closer underneath us with almost no movement. As if it were all coincidental and they couldn't see us at all. I can feel my adrenaline levels rising and my pulse increasing.

Mara has made a deep dive and is searching for lang-oustine by poking in the cracks of the reef. Suddenly the largest of the three predators breaks away from the orbit, increases speed and heads for the unidentified being that is Mara. Just to see if it is something edible perhaps. At the same time Tawake heads straight downwards and creates as much commotion as is possible underwater: jerking his arms, banging the corals with his spear, screaming through bubbles. The shark, irritated, stops and turns back. It is only now that Mara notices what has been happening behind his back. Quickly, but intentionally calmly, the two swim to the top. In the short moment in which the shark stopped almost right next to Mara, I had a chance to estimate its length: a good 2.5 metres.

Our canoe has been anchored an endless 150 metres away. We decide to wait first and scramble onto the peak of the Tower. Every so often we peek over the edge to scan the depths. At one point we can see six dark shadows floating above the light sand. Mara explains: 'Those are *Qio Kata*, blacktip reef sharks. They wait for the low tide and the fish that swim out through the passage with it. If there are several, they can become unpleasant. They become like a gang and gain courage. On their own they are completely harmless.'

Harmless! I'm becoming sick of hearing the word: 'You said there are hardly any sharks here and now it is swarming with them down there!' Tawake grins: 'Would you have come along if we had said anything else? It's such a good fishing place. And anyway, we will take care of you.'

This means that we have to kill time by collecting mussels and only start swimming toward the canoe after an hour when the tide starts falling. Not a shark in sight; and yet, those 150 metres did drag on.

In the evening we discuss the day's events. The daily colour explosion at sunset has ended and the high feathery clouds have removed their golden angel's robes again. The sky, lagoon and the beach are dipped in a transparent blue. The first stars appear in the sky. The day has ended. This is the hour to celebrate the evening, to sing, tell stories and feel good.

The meeting house is stuffy. We carry the *tanoa*, the sticky, four-footed wooden bowl outside and spread mats on the grass. The young men mix *kava* powder with water to make *yaqona*, the national drink of the Pacific. After the first round has been ceremonially served and drunk according to Fijian etiquette, the mood lightens up. Conversations begin, guitars and ukuleles are tuned.

We tell the story of our shark adventure, at great length and elaborately embellished, just the way people like it in these parts. When we finish, white-haired, weather-beaten Nathanieli, the senior chief and keeper of tradition, the *Custom*, says pensively and with quiet reprimand: 'Chris couldn't know this, but Tawake and Mara, you should have: since the old days our clan animal has been the shark. We pay the sharks respect and we can call them. We have never captured a shark, as it is done on other islands. That is why a shark has never attacked our people. We are under their protection. You could have swum back to the canoe without worrying.'

Tawake and Mara remain silent. I can feel their scepticism. Debating with the old man or disputing his statement would be an insult to the *Custom*. And respecting the *Custom* is the highest law in a Fijian village.

We smoke, drink coconut shells of *yaqona*, we sing. Suddenly the dogs in the village begin to bark hysterically. The conversation comes to an abrupt end. Everyone listens attentively into the darkness. Eventually one of the men says tersely: '*Veli*.' – 'It's the *Velis*, no doubt. The dogs have got a whiff of the *Velis*.' The others confirm, nod concurringly with a knowing look. The tension slowly subsides and conversations pick up again. They have found a new old topic, an endless one.

'The *Velis*? What are they?' I ask with a feigned naivety. The men turn toward me with excited expressions: 'Does the *Vulagi* not know all gripping stories about the *Velis*? How wonderful!' Chief Isireli, my host and Tawake and Mara's father, takes it upon himself to enlighten me. He puts on his most enigmatic face, sits down with his legs crossed and begins: 'The *Velis* are the little people from the forest. They were already on the island before our ancestors arrived with their large double canoes. In those days they owned all of the land. But the *Velis* aren't warriors. So when the tall people came, they retreated into the forests. No one knows how many there are because the forests are so dense and there are so many islands that are uninhabited. – In the evening twilight we can often hear them sing and laugh, up in the bush. Many of our songs come from them. If they like someone because he has done something good for them, they will sometimes give him one of their songs as a gift.'

'And what do the *Velis* look like?' I ask.

'As a young man I saw a *Veli* for the first time. It was like this: I was in the bush hunting wild boar when the dogs suddenly began growling. I looked into the woods and there, right next to a tree a little man stood still. He wasn't wearing any clothing and had fur like an animal. His eyes were deep and he spoke to me with them. For a long time. He had *Mana*, the Power, I could feel it. When I moved he turned around and ran away silently.'

'So they are friendly?'

'If you are friendly to them. But woe betide anyone who insults them. For instance by cutting down one of their sacred trees. Then they will plague you for a long time. They will hide your tools, tear up your nets, traumatise your dogs ... one should always remain on good terms with them.'

It was the same story. Admittedly, I had pretended to be naïve. Ever since I began travelling on the islands, I have collected *Veli*-stories. From Kadavu in the south to Vanua Levu in the north and from Yasawas in the west to the Lau Islands in the east; everyone in Fiji knows about the little people in the forest. Perhaps a collective memory of an ancient pygmy civilisation that may still exist in small numbers? Or 'just' the South Sea version of mythical fairies, elves and gnomes found the world over? Even ethnologists are puzzled by this question. I didn't see any *Velis* on my travels. But even so, the dogs reacted to something. I can confirm that much.

The senior chief seems to be well-disposed toward me. He invites me to visit him in his beach hut. The old magician withdraws to this place outside the village to meditate, compose *mekes*, Fijian songs and dances, or to write the great dance ballads that the whole village will help enact. In order to create such a performance everyone will spend several weeks rehearsing rigorously during the hour before sunset and follow all of the chief's strict directions. Once it is dark I take a lantern and make my way along the narrow path to Nathanieli's little cove so that I can hear the old myths and legends from him. They are the tales of the giant twins, the devil who had to give his ability to walk on fire to the inhabitants of the island of Beqa, the crying princess Tagimauthia whose tears turned into blossoms, the powerful snake *Dengei* and … and … and … So many islands, so many stories, thousands of them. And even across a distance of thousands of nautical miles, people tell the same stories across the entire Pacific. Still. In the evening when the sun has set. Or someone puts the 'Rambo' cassette into the video player.

Now I have to say goodbye. After nearly three months in 'my' village on 'my' island. I celebrated their festivals, of which I enjoyed the occasion for giving thanks to mat weaving the most. It is organised solely by the men. They set up, decorate, cook, serve, dance and sing. It is to show their gratitude for the work the women do throughout the year. I respected Sunday rest, like all the other devoted inhabitants and spent it endlessly bored because it is not permitted

to do anything that day other than go to church –
no swimming, no ballgames, no nothing. I levered
the heavy taro-roots out of the mud in the swamps of
the spring valley with a stick, beat breadfruit out of
the treetops, carried banana tree shrubs along narrow
paths into the village, waited for the little fish to bite
in the reef under the sparkling night sky, hunted wild
boar with bamboo spears and machetes … I got to
know what it means to be part of a community, to live
the 'simple life' in which everyone needs the others in
order to live together and not adjacent to one another.
Perhaps I didn't *just* get to know this. Maybe I really
did learn it.

When I look back at my time on the island I
wonder what it was that had the deepest impact on
me. I think it must have been the hurricane. The
resulting experience of closeness, togetherness and
care overwhelmed me more than witnessing a breathtaking natural phenomenon.

The days at the beginning of November were
hot and humid. The enormous old mango trees up
on the hills above the village were heavily weighed

down by their autumnal load. The bulging red-yellow lacquered fruits hung close together pulling the branches down. Some of the over-ripe harvest fell to the ground during the short but intense showers and quickly began to ferment in the moist heat. Hundreds of metallic shining butterflies, the size of plates, drank themselves into a stupor from the fruit mash and only flew into the air clumsily when lightly pushed. The sweet sticky scent of liquor lay heavy on the land. There was no refreshing trade wind from the ocean, not even the smallest breath of wind for days. The ebb-dry lagoon stank of rot and iodine.

'Hurricane weather, I have a feeling … we ought to listen to the radio', mumbled Isireli and eyed up the veiled, murky horizon in the west. Isireli's feeling was right. Only a day later, 'Fiji One' reported a depression north-west of the island group. A few hours later it intensified into a hurricane which marched straight for us with a constantly growing force.

As if the storm had been waiting for this official meteorological announcement, the first gusts of wind started sweeping into the cove right after the radio warning, making the palms dance. Isireli gathered the village together and delegated tasks: secure the wood houses with cables, board up doors and windows, knock as many nuts off the palm trees in the village as possible (they could become lethal missiles), herd the pigs into the pens, tie up the canoes on land, fill all available containers with spring water, cook an emergency supply of food, prepare the basement of the church. Who should do what with whom. Then go!

No one was hectic. Everyone went to work full of élan and positive happy energy. Conscientious activity, encouraging calls to the others, laughter all around. Even the smallest children pitched in, provided they could walk. They chased the chickens and ducks into their enclosure with earnest faces, carried blankets to the church, and collected firewood. The village was a well-trained team – as if they had practised for this emergency many times, the way a ship's crew regularly carries out lifeboat drill.

Most of the houses in the village were still the beautiful old kind made of logs, bamboo walls and thick reed roofs in the style of the classic Bures. They could withstand a mid-strength storm. The light wood houses with corrugated iron roofs, bizarrely named 'European Houses', would probably not cope as well. The pan-Pacific breeze block had not yet found its foothold on the island. Even the church was airy, made of wood with many windows (and decorated with three large clocks and two made in Taiwan Leonardo-Last-Supper-Tapestries). Only the large basement was made from cement so that it could fulfil its current purpose whenever it was needed; namely providing a shelter for about 150 villagers. The hurricane which the meteorologists had named Uma was now only four hours away. The countdown had begun. Wind was already roaring through the treetops and beating the lagoon into a white froth.

We all sat together huddled on mats in the dim, low room. The pastor had given a small speech, we sang and prayed. Now we were concentrating on listening to the unmoved voice in the crackling transistor: Uma was moody, she briefly devastated the west of the main island and was now sweeping over the ocean with added strength, looking for victims. It was our turn now, despite the fact that the centre of the storm was expected to rage several miles from the coast. We might just get away without serious damage. *Might* ...

The flare-up of individual squalls transformed into a constant screaming with a whimpering whistle accompanying as a soprano. Outside, the apocalypse was taking place: the rain was whipping past almost horizontally, broken twigs sweeping through the air, the small corrugated-iron hut for copra drying folded up with a clang, coconut palms lay on top of each other in a mess and the lagoon, which looked like a dark overflowing mass, flooded into the village. Dirty rags of froth licked at the foundations of the lower houses. The air tasted salty. Murky scraps of clouds raced from horizon to horizon as if in fast-forward. The sky was falling on our heads. All we could hope for was that the church wouldn't do the same. The sound of creaking, scraping, groaning and squeaking in the rafters above us certainly was worrying. It went on like this for hours.

And then, unexpectedly, it seemed like someone slowly but constantly turned down the volume on the gigantic Dolby-Surround-System, and the spectacle subsided, just like that. Uma had lost her motivation. Even rain dribbled to the ground, worn out. The island lay exhausted and in disarray. Worn out but happy to have escaped the worst, we climbed out into the open and look at the outcome of the last hours. It could have been worse.

The next day we began cleaning up – as a team. One week later the only evidence of Uma's passing were the shredded palm trees. Admittedly we wouldn't be picking any more mangoes this year, as Uma had thoroughly harvested the lot.

Yes, our little hurricane really was quite impressive. Partly because after the last few days I spent preparing the village, sharing shelter underground, fixing the damages with the others, I really belonged to this community. I had been accepted and that is a great feeling.

And so now I have to say goodbye. How can I do such a thing? On my last morning as we sit on the mats at sunrise drinking Early-Morning-Tea, conversation simply won't take off. Nathanieli does his best by telling a long anecdote about his time in the Pacific War up in the Solomon Islands. He soon gives up. It's no use.

Isireli, Tawake and Mara accompany me to the main island. That makes my departure a little easier. It is bad enough either way. The only way I can bear it is by knowing that I will come back. Everyone is at the beach: Wainimere, Demua, Vela, Patemo, Josefa, Osea, Nathanieli, the entire village. As a last good bye we sing *Isa Lei*, the Fijian farewell song ('Don't forget us now, when you are far away ...').

The worryingly overloaded village boat slowly moves out of the lagoon with its ancient motor sputtering. We are bringing six goats to the market, bundles of taro-roots and two buckets of freshwater crabs. Eventually the panorama of soft green hilltops, bizarre cone-shaped volcanoes and wide beaches melts into a floating blue vision between water and sky. Framed by the white foam wreaths of the surf other islands drift across the horizon like flawless sandy bulges covered in a few straggly palm trees leaning against the Trade Wind. They slide past and move in front of our island.

Isireli and his sons want to buy a new outboard motor on Suva. This is an important, well-planned operation, since they only come here, to Fiji's enormous capital city (90,000 inhabitants) once a year at most. It is a totally different world. Cars, traffic lights, zebra crossing, houses with three or more storeys, cinemas, bars, the impressive government district, the sprawling university campus, the port, the cruise ships, the futuristic container terminal …

After weeks on the island without electricity or car horns and the loudest noise being that of the parrots screeching in the forest, the city really knocks me out. Does everything really have to be so fast and noisy? We shuffle through the big city bustle as a tightly packed group of wide-eyed provincial outsiders looking to each other for protection. I am supposed to join them while they shop. The merchant is Indian and no Fijian trusts an Indian. Presumably the white man will come in handy as a referee in this situation.

As pitiful as it sounds, even now *and* after 27 years of independence, mistrust, prejudice and alienation still dominate relations between the two largest population groups of the prospering island state which consist of 398,000 native Fijians and 343,000 citizens of Indian origin, descending from the plantation workers brought in by British colonial landowners at the turn of the century.

The Indian vendor – Vinod Patel Fishing Gear and Outboard Motors Limited – turns out to be a serious and conciliatory business partner. Even Isireli has to agree. He puts it down to my presence. I can tell that there is no use in trying to argue. On our last day we go to the photographer. This must happen as it is an important ritual. Pronab Maganlal – Master of Photography – is also Indian. In his little courtyard studio he serves us with professional graciousness. Again, Isireli puts it down to my presence. No, there is really no use in arguing with him …

We do not sing *Isa Lei* at the airport. Tawake and Mara hand me a small, newspaper-wrapped parcel and we try to finish our farewell with as much dignity as possible. '*Sa mothe, tuaka-na,* and come back soon!'

'Of course I will be back, *sa mothe* and *vinaka vakalevu!*'

On the flight to Rarotonga I unwrap the parcel: It is a large shark's tooth with a hole drilled into it and a beautifully plaited coconut fibre cord. The headline on the page of newspaper announces 'Fiji – the way the world should be'. Whether this is true or not, I will certainly becoming back.

The Voyage of the Ai Sokula
A Pacific log book

Cast off was designated at eight in the evening. It was written in white chalk on the blackboard that lists all the incoming and outgoing ships. 'But don't forget: Fiji time' the employee of Wong's Shipping Company had added and raised his eyebrows with a smile. This is a gesture many people in these parts use to emphasise important information. Yes of course, local time in Fiji, what else? 'Fiji time' is a highly variable time-stretching factor that a foreigner will only understand and begin to estimate and apply after spending several weeks in this 300-island-state. I should probably learn it quickly.

When I arrive in the port half an hour before departure time (just to be on the safe side) the cranes between the quay and the loading hatch of the aged freight liner are still busily swinging back and forth. The height of the cargo heaps on deck suggests that this may go on for another few hours. Fiji time? 'Not before midnight' Captain Patemo confirms after briefly, critically but not impolitely inspecting me amidst the general chaos and then taking my bag into storage and advising me to spend a nice last evening at Lucky Eddie's. Why my last?

The old *Ai Sokula* really isn't a ship to inspire much faith. And certainly not pretty, more like a sister-ship of the *Yorrike*, Traven's fictional 'Death Ship': it has a black rust-streaked hull, a superstructure that used to (a *long* time ago) be white, an aged refrigeration container clumsily positioned in front of the wheelhouse, dented metal barrels tightly packed one next to the other. But somehow the whole thing feels cosy. This will be my home for the next two or three weeks. If I do embark on this journey. Right now I could still turn back.

But simply the names of the islands win me over with their pure South Sea feeling: Vanualévu, Tavéuni, Lauthála, Jatháta, Naitáumba, Kanathéa, Thikómbia-i-Lau, Vanuambalávu, Susúi, Mángo and Thítia. The sacrifice of certain comforts is worth what awaits me – a round trip through the northern Lau Islands. There is no better way to get to know these islands as there are hardly any landing strips and no tourism. Why would one want to go there if one has no business being there? The only reason can be the strong urge to get to know all of this oceanic country with its hundreds of islands across endless breadths of the ocean – at least as well as a traveller from the other world can. And because one is so easily infected by the endearing openness that Fijians show towards foreigners, by their self-confident way of life and their impressive culture. Because these islands and their people are irresistible.

The *Ai Sokula* it is, then. One of many cargo ships that help maintain the unity between Fiji's peripheral island groups and the commercial centre in the city of Suva on Viti Levu, she delivers diesel for generators, gasoline for boat motors, cement, corrugated iron and reinforced steel, as well as sugar, rice and tea, washing powder, soap and razor blades. In short, all types of consumer goods from sewing machines to radio batteries to lollipops for the kids. Yes, those are necessary too.

Half an hour before midnight I return to the port – just to be on the safe side. I had used my spare time to buy some provisions and gifts (just in case): radio batteries, corned beef, biscuits, cigarettes and apples, an imported delicacy from New Zealand. The busy crowd is milling about in the bright floodlights in front of the ship; it seems that all the passengers and the large families of the crew members have finally assembled below. They ask where on earth I have been all this time since they have all been waiting and could have left port a long time ago! I now under-stand that Fiji Time does not just stretch in one direc-tion. Sometimes, very rarely but nonetheless, things even happen at their designated time and no one can quite figure out how this could have happened. Of course it takes nearly an hour before everyone who ought to be is on board and everyone who just came aboard to say goodbye has left.

The previously empty afterdeck has now turned into a chaotic and crowded camp. Reed mats are rolled out all along the railings and there are colourful floral blankets and pillows spread out all over them. Among other things there are also baskets, suitcases, large plastic containers, stacked cardboard boxes, bundles of taro, and heaps of bananas, kava and coconuts. (Why people constantly transport coconuts from one place to another in a country that is covered in coconut palms remains a mystery of the Pacific.) The mood is that of a fun-fair or picnic and the stranger is naturally welcomed by everyone. Too bad I booked one of the only two cabins on board. It is more expensive, tiny, humid and musty but now there is also no more space left on deck.

Travelling the Pacific requires a proper degree of fatalism. Osea Namua has enough of it. He also has a deck of playing cards, a guitar and an inexhaustible repertoire of songs and good humour. The young teacher is on his way to Kanathéa with his wife and child to be headmaster there. If there were a direct connection between the two islands, the family could make it to its destination within a day. Since their island is only sixth on the route, they will spend four days on board the ship with their boxes and bags and one crate containing three happily squealing piglets. It is more than possible that the trip could take two or three days longer if there is a storm or the captain receives radio orders to stop at an additional island. '*Waka Malau*,' Osea says and raises his eyebrows with a smile, 'that's just how it is'.

The *Ai Sokula* slowly pushes her way through Harbour Bay heading for the passage in the surrounding reef. Suva's lamps shrink to a thin blinking chain of fairy lights in the darkness. The night is warm, calm, and cloudless and the stars sparkling in the night seem close enough to touch. The first flying fish are spraying across the water in front of the bow as daybreak announces itself.

At some point during my second night I sense some commotion on deck. I half-hear strange noises, footsteps and calls. The ship's propeller stops. I sit up with a fright. I knew it, the engine is damaged, what else, on this godforsaken ship! Or maybe we have run aground on a reef because of the tipsy dilettantes who are navigating us! There certainly had been a suspicious number of beer bottles lying about on the bridge earlier. And the Koro Sea is notorious for its precarious reefs. Not to mention the many sharks. I just knew it! All of a sudden I am wide awake.

Then I hear it. And this is a new sound; one that I can't place among the range of those I have already grown accustomed to on board. The hull is clanging. It is clicking and chirping and squeaking. There are voices speaking outside. Confused, I pull myself together and climb upstairs. Everyone is standing together on the afterdeck and looking out onto the night sea – spellbound. The water is calm under the full moon and the small waves are forming a regular glinting pattern on the surface. The light is silver and silence surrounds us. Apart from the singing voices coming from the hull. Or from the depths of the sea.

We are surrounded. A pod of small whales is playing all around the old *Ai Sokula*. Dark square heads, sighing sprays of breath, slapping tails, elegant rising followed by elegiac curves sinking under again. And everywhere we look we can see swelling backs ploughing back and forth through the water. All in a strange colourless light. Most striking are their voices in the silence: the whales are singing and speaking to each other. Rather than hearing it with our ears, we are feeling and hearing it through our feet, rising through our bodies and filling our heads. The ship is vibrating like an underwater sounding-board. Good vibrations. And yet, we can't understand them, let alone respond to them. The whales have taken us into their midst. Have they accepted us? All we can do is stand, look and listen.

Eventually – the next morning no one knows how long we were captivated by the enchantment – all of the many whales sank back into the deep, perhaps they were tired of not getting a response from us. Captain Patemo sighs, raises his eyebrows, smiles apologetically and gives orders for the engines to be started again.

'This vessel is a mess', Iliseri, the first officer, comments sarcastically. It is not an apology but a mere statement of fact. And he is right: the ship is a complete pigsty and we are like a grimy bunch of bachelors. If someone really insists on showering, he will have to pick the debris out of the drain in the only functioning bath on board. And if someone needs a spoon then he'll just have to rinse one in the galley (if he thinks it's really necessary to use a clean one). So what?

One compartment, however, is always proper, tidy and spotless: the bridge is no laughing matter. The dark veneer always shines, the brass fittings sparkle and the windows are spotless. The compass is floating in its glass sphere; the large wooden steering wheel is in the centre, the engine telegraph is looking antiquated and everything is as nostalgic as it is effective. This is the pride of the entire crew.

What nights I spent on the bridge, travelling the Koro Sea from one island to the next! Everyone who can't sleep turns up here at some point and looks out onto the dark sea far beyond the bow. Conversations drip drop sluggishly. The *Ai Sokula*, our home, our little world, trudges ahead tirelessly while somewhere islands drift past us. If we spot the glint of a light beyond the reef, the sensation of life is so overwhelming we can discuss it for hours. Out there amongst the expanse of water a relative lives, or a school friend or someone else. People know each other out here. It is both a tiny and an enormous country: 700,000 inhabitants, 300 islands, of which only half are populated, spread across a half a million square kilometres, which consist of over 90 per cent water. But those are just numbers ... I have never experienced more timeless times than here. Never have I felt so at home as in the nights on the old *Ai Sokula*.

My favourite place to watch, read and write during the day is – depending on the wind and weather conditions either starboard or port – on one of the two little balconies of the outer bridge. There is a little bench by the railing, one can chat to the helmsman in the bridge house through the open door and the view over the front of the ship is better than anywhere else on board. My reading is a lovely Diederich edition of *Moby Dick*, as this is the ultimate book about the Pacific. Correspondingly the title of the 111th chapter is 'The Pacific'. The portrayal of the ocean on two pages in this chapter belongs to the most beautiful of his prose; Herman Melville writes:

> There is, one knows not what sweet
> mystery about this sea, whose gently
> awful stirrings seem to speak of some
> hidden soul beneath; like those fabled
> undulations of the Ephesian sod over the
> buried Evangelist St. John. And meet it is,
> that over these sea-pastures, wide-rolling
> watery prairies and Potters' Fields of all
> four continents, the waves should rise and
> fall, and ebb and flow unceasingly; for here,
> millions of mixed shades and shadows,
> drowned dreams, somnambulisms,
> reveries; all that we call lives and souls,
> lie dreaming, dreaming, still; tossing like
> slumberers in their beds; the ever-rolling
> waves but made so by their restlessness.
>
> To any meditative Magian rover, this
> serene Pacific, once beheld, must ever

after be the sea of his adoption. It rolls the
midmost waters of the world, the Indian
ocean and Atlantic being but its arms.

Hour upon hour can be spent looking out on the
wide rolling swell without seeing anything else but
the ocean; barely moving rippling silver or deep blue
with chasing white foam tips, dull grey and heavy
or translucent shining. The endless expanse in infi-
nite variations is always in motion and above it the
unfeigned sky. But other than that: nothing. And
yet, not a day passes without an extraordinary maritime encounter; the watery desert is alive. Once we
pass a large brown and yellow turtle that watches our
movement with an outstretched neck and little interest. Once, the sea ahead suddenly begins to bubble
and tiny fish spray across the wave in silver sparks.
A school of barracudas or tuna is hunting a swarm of
sardines that has risen out of the depths like a cloud.
In the blink of an eye the sky is filled with countless screaming, circling seabirds that are all plunging
greedily into the water.

Much more exciting than that were the two sharks that followed the ship patiently for hours. During the day there are always a few fishing lines with bait dragging behind the stern – even at full steam – and rarely a day passes without a tuna biting. This is what our friends are waiting for. The important thing is to reel the line in at top speed as soon as one bites, before the sharks can get to it. This doesn't always work. Right under the stern one of the big grey creatures catches up with the yellowfin, turns on its back and bites down hard. Two-thirds for him, one-third left for us. At least we have managed to save the precious hook and have tuna curry for dinner.

The most fascinating spectacle offered by the sea takes place on dark nights when pale glowing clouds rise from the depths and float and circle, pulsating like giant jellyfish a few metres under the surface. 'Millions of mixed shades and shadows, drowned dreams, somnambulisms, reveries … ' There is no doubt that the seafaring Melville often marvelled at these phosphorescent clouds of plankton.

Bola, our supercargo, comes on board with a Lee's-cabin-crackers-tin under his arm. It is a present from the village we have anchored at today. He drops his load on the afterdeck. There is a loud rattling inside the tin canister. He grins and says 'Look at them, aren't they nice?' and pulls out his booty: they are two blue-green shelled, plate-sized coconut crabs. They are slowly rowing their impressive pincers back and forth, foaming at the mouth. It is said that at night they climb onto palm trees, cut the nuts off, climb down again, crack the hard shell open and then feast on the flesh. The islanders call them palm thieves and nail protective metal collars around the trunks of the trees. They say that these creatures could easily cut through a finger, slowly and remorselessly. I am filled with respect.

They also say, however, that these crabs are a delicacy. A pot of water is brought to a boil in the galley. A short while later all of the people on watch below are standing gathered around the anchor capstan. One axe, one metal bowl, a few cooked taro roots as a side dish and a bottle of Fiji Bitter and the feast can begin – cutlery won't be necessary.

The slimy, green and yellow flesh inside the crab shells looks so awful it makes me want to vomit. I would never eat such a thing voluntarily, never! But the right to hospitality and therefore also the duty to hospitality is sacred in Fiji. So here I go! It tastes … fantastic, on a par with lobster and caviar. We eat gobble, dip, suck and lick our fingers.

At night we travel and during the daytime we work. This is the normal rhythm of the copra freighters in the Pacific. We travel to twenty islands in three weeks. Hardly any of them have passages in the surrounding coral reefs that are wide and deep enough for the ship to pass through into the lagoon. So we anchor out on the roadstead, swing out the longboat, move aside the planks over the hold, the derrick squeaks and rattles into action and the freight determined for each specific island is lifted out of the ship with large nets, lowered onto the boat and taken on land.

It sounds simple but can also turn into a real thrill when we approach islands that are surrounded by a reef that has no entry passage whatsoever. A solid, uninterrupted barrier made of razor-sharp corals, an underwater wreath of a wall, on top of which the waves crash thunderously. This then means we have to wait and get as close as possible to the rearing swell until a wave comes that is high enough to carry the heavily-laden longboat over the reef. And this has to happen more than just once. It may well be that there are ten boatloads worth of copra on the beach. And our job is, after all, to get all of it and 'empty the isle'.

This is where Bola comes in. After the captain, he is the most important man on board. Half of our trip's success depends on his business sense, experience and negotiation skills. As soon as we hit land, he starts snooping through the copra sheds like a hound, crumbling some dried coconut flesh in his hands, poking his nose between a pile of jute sacks with a disgusted expression on his face and so on. And soon he knows everything: this is good, mature, fat merchandise, or: this is already beginning to rot because a rainstorm soaked the copra in the middle of its drying process. Bola decides the price.

In the evening, after work, we all sit together on the afterdeck drinking *jaqona* and singing. We are a loyal band far away from the rest of the world, under the Pacific night sky. Next to us is a small island, its palm trees are rustling in the wind. Slowly and silently black bats, flying foxes the size of crows glide down from the mountains into the fruit orchards. In the lagoon, fish are jumping near the surface making slapping sounds and the night-time hunting and being hunted has begun. The kerosene lamp is hissing. We are singing. Three stripped guitars, one battered ukulele and a dozen sonorous male voices, instantly split into a four-part harmony, professional and highly musical. And tearjerkingly wonderful. Or maybe just totally kitschy. How was I to know, being completely caught up in it. So we were singing.

As an acoustic provision, I have brought along a complete recording of *The Magic Flute*. At some point one of them listened to my walkman headphones, pulled up his eyebrows and clicked his tongue. Now everyone wants to hear what this is all about. The cassette is placed into the ghetto blaster and Mozart does the talking, there under the Pacific starlit sky, far away from the rest of the world.

The overture plays. There is little reaction except for the slow ebbing of conversation. It's just European music, very jumbled and far too many instruments. The first act. Tamino's appearance, the snake, the three ladies: 'Help, help, or else I am lost ...' From that moment on we sit up attentively, our legs crossed, listening for one and a half hours. The moon wanders across the sky. The palm trees rustle. A tired-out rooster crows. Schikaneder's old, naively complicated story tells itself, Mozart's eternally young music shines. The arias of the Queen of the Night and Sarastro's 'Heil'ge Hallen' are applauded with tongue clicks and raised eyebrows.

During the passages containing dialogue I have to explain the plot – 'what's going on now?' – and then provide a brief summary of 250 years of opera history. To them it means little, after all: a theatre, a stage at the front, an orchestra below, stage sets, all of it together ... They have never heard of it. They do, however, all know the cinemas in the capital city: Ah, so it's like a film with living people. So basically a *Meke*, the Fijian song and dance festival. It all makes sense now.

The following night the crew members who were on watch the night before want to hear *The Magic Flute*. Expertly, Nathanieli, the second officer explains: 'Listen! Now the curtain rises, and there's a deep forest, and you see *Dengei*, the big snake, am I right Chris?'(Somehow it is self-understood that they switch from Fijian to English as soon as I'm around. Sensitivity and consideration never struck me as a typical qualities of a sailor … it must be a Fijian thing.)

As I am falling asleep that same night I can hear *Magic Flute* melodies being played on the guitar and ukulele with a South Sea sweetening and a dark Melanesian flavour added. In the next few days the themes are played over and over again, adapted and amalgamated. Soon there are also lyrics; after all South Sea music is based on song. Nathanieli tries to translate: the son of Tongan nobility falls in love with an ordinary girl and both families have been in a feud for generations. The lovers have to flee and find shelter in a cave. Montagues and Capulets, Romeo and Julia, Tamino and Pamina, love and pain. The happy ending takes place in Fijian exile nearby. It is a popular love story in these parts, an old legend. Schikaneder and Mozart would have loved it.

Fiji closes down on the weekend. The Fijians firmly believe in upholding the values that the white light-bringers from far away *Beritani* drummed into them 150 years ago. So, Sunday is a day where nothing happens. With the exception of a minimum of two church services – nothing at all. No football, no dancing, no swimming and certainly no unloading of cargo. All these things and many others are of the devil. Consequently the old *Ai Sokula* has been moored at a small rain-forest pier since Saturday – whether we like it or not. We, who are self-confessed agnostics or practising sinners, however, quietly lower the longboat into the water and row out to the reef. We hang two bright kerosene lamps over the edge in order to attract the prey and loosely hold plastic lines between thumb and forefinger with crab-meat on hooks at the end. We now have more than enough time for long conversations elaborate tales. Our favourite topic: *Ka vuni ni wasawasa*, the endless ocean and its many secrets.

There is a sudden commotion. Below us a swarm of barracudas is circling and biting at the bait wildly. Hectic activity breaks out. The line is pulled in with fast, wide arm movements, someone grips the fish behind its gills, bludgeons its head, releases the hook, puts more bait on it and throws it back into the water. This will give us supplies for days. Then suddenly all is calm again and the swarm has moved on. The swell is rocking the boat; above us millions of light splinters are turning in the black velvet sky.

As we are rowing back I spot these yellow glowing eyes directly on the surface of the water. My companions let out screams, which although they are muted are very alarmed: it is a large octopus. All atavistic hunting instincts immediately kick in. Every man in this country, whether he is a tax inspector or a civil engineer, is still also a farmer or a fisherman and in the layer beneath that a hunter and gatherer. Despite having been internalised, the ambivalent and forced process of adapting to 'Western civilisation' took place little more than three generations ago.

Captain Patemo, who normally reminds me of

Folco Lulli in *The Wages of Fear* – small, compact, muscular, pot-bellied and shrewd – is now taking on the form of Gregory Peck in the role of Captain Ahab. So: Captain Folco Gregory Patemo is standing on the bow and reaches for the grappling hook. The boat is slowly drifting toward the dark, staring head around which the water is curling in loops. He takes on big swing and hits the target. Pat pulls the lance with the prey on it out of the water at lightning speed and in that same moment there is an eruption of flying tentacles, beating and slapping all over Pat's body. Before he is knocked down or out of the boat, the other rush to his aid, pulling the octopus' limbs off of him one sucker after another, with a lot of smacking and whirling noises. Immediately the snaking arms have suctioned onto another body part, everyone in the bow is wrestling, groaning almost silently, the boat is swaying precariously, filling with water, the men stab and cut with their knives, a gruesome massacre, I'm sitting almost paralysed on my rowing bench. The thoughts shooting through my mind are 'Laocoon live!' and 'No one at home will ever believe this.'

Eventually it is all over. This will provide food for weeks since the octopus can be smoked, frozen, sold on the next island and increase our meagre pay as a result. Allegedly they haven't caught a *Kuitangolo* this big for years. The arms are nearly two metres long (and will grow over the next few days) and the others ask me whether I would like to keep the beak as a souvenir.

We have an unexpected day off. The *Ai Sokula* is bobbing on the roadstead in front of the jungle pier of Waiyevo. We have to wait for the Government freighter to discharge its load at the pier: futuristic segments of a gigantic dish antenna for a telegraph station. Iliseri, Bola, Nathanieli and Osea decide to take me on a journey; the *Kai Jiamani*, the guest from Germany must to be introduced to the beautiful attractions of Taveuni, most certainly!

We rent an ancient pickup truck at the gas station in the village; buy plenty of provisions in the shop and take off on our men's trip. The unpaved road snakes up and downhill wildly, most of the time just along the part rocky, part white sand beach framed coastline. We drive through untouched rainforests, past the glittering threads of narrow waterfalls, through wide open coconut plantations with blonde cows grazing in them. To our right the velvet green mountainside rises more than 1,000 metres high, to our left the view opens out onto a turquoise and jade shimmering lagoon, with the white foam strips of surf on the reef and the deep blue surface of the Somosomo Strait behind it. The 80-kilometre coastal road of Taveuni would no doubt reach the shortlist in a The-most-beautiful-roads-on-this-earth-contest. It is a landscape of breathtaking beauty. 'The garden island of Fiji' is what Taveuni, the greenest island in the archipelago, is called.

Our destination is the Bouma Waterfall. 'The most beautiful spot on earth,' Nathanieli assures me as if he knew all the famous waterfalls on earth intimately. But he is right: it is a magical niche far away from the rest of the world, a place for fairies, mermaids and unicorns and I have loved it since I first swam in the little rock pool under the rushing cascade at the end of the deep forest valley several years ago.

But it would be impossible to tell them this since it is so important to them to show me their country at its very best. As we turn around the last bend and I can see waterfall, pool, stream, fern trees and hibiscus bushes in the shade and sun flickering they look at me full of expectation, like parents opening the door to the Christmas presents for their children. And I don't even have to pretend: the magic works just as it had before.

We swim in the ice-cold current of the waterfall, go fishing for crabs in the streams and roast them on the fire. We wander through the forest, cut down coconuts from the trees, have a nap on the grass and go for another swim. There are no problems in our lives, the world is wide. Far away. Everything is easy. A green glowing day, as if Gauguin had painted it.

When we return to the ship in the evening we can already hear them from far away. 'Empty tin makes much noise', Nathanieli growls. They have also had their day off. Now they are all in good spirits and working in a busy jumble to prepare a *lovo*, which is a type of earth oven. A hole has been dug in the pebble beach and inside it a strong wood fire is burning with large stones heating on top of it. Meanwhile the dishes of fish, chicken, Cassava tubers, taro-pudding – all flavoured with *lolo*, the thick milk of grated and pressed coconuts – have been wrapped and tied into handy banana-leaf parcels. When the fire has burnt down, the stone slabs are rolled apart and the green parcels are placed in between and covered with a thick layer of leaves and earth. This then steams away for about one hour and slowly a range of seductive smells spreads out across the beach. It is a gargantuan Pacific feast by the light of the kerosene lamp on the jetty between land and sea. Later – of course – the evening continues with guitars and ukuleles playing many long, melancholic, desire-filled songs until late into the night.

In the early morning, shortly after sunrise, we carefully grope our way through a gargling passage into the wide atoll of the Exploring Islands. A fine film of drizzle veils the scenery. It is chilly. To the left I can see a chain of small and larger islands, hilly and green, lined with palm trees. Across the expanse of calm water there are more islands, in soft focus from the rain behind the lagoon lake. A large group of islands. A lot of cargo, a lot of copra to handle, a full day of work, at least. We moor on the pier of the main island of Vanuambalavu. In front of us spread across a large piece of grassland is a large village. An old missionary church, quince-yellow under a red pitched roof, next to it the Government Station, hospital, post office, boarding school, copra co-operative: Lomaloma, the administrative centre of the Northern Lau Group.

The villagers begin to stream in, the Chinese shop-keeper's pickup truck rattles up. The arrival of the ship is a special day; news, cash, goods for the store (the island has probably been waiting weeks for cigarettes, sugar, rice ...). The last passengers say goodbye. To the disappointment of the crew, sweet Losalini, the young nurse with the irresistible smile for whom we all would have done anything, is also getting off here; Bola is useless for the next few days. For the remaining third of the journey, the twelve-man crew is on its own. Except for the *Kai Jiamani*. But he has long felt accepted by them – and this is certainly not just because he has always tried to lend an overzealous but clumsy hand on board. (Ought he to sit there idly and watch them work? How boring.)

The boards over the cargo hold are moved to the side as yet another day of work begins. Pat, the laid back, lethargic boozer is like a new man; he is full of unfamiliar energy and restlessness and urging the crew to hurry up. Hurry up?! Captain Patemo, a Fijian! The men grumble but are amused and put their noses to the grindstone. He must have a good reason. In the evening, when the cargo derrick has lowered the last copra sack into the ship, the chief reveals his reason: Pat comes from Susui, the neighbouring island visible from here and the inhabitants are hosting a *Meke* (a song and dance fest) in his and our honour there tonight. We simply have to go.

As soon as the last board has been replaced, the old *Ai Sokula* sputters across the lagoon. Meanwhile there is intense activity going on in the shower and under the water hose. We are searching for our least dirty shirts, slapping on generous amounts of aftershave. The captain has donated two crates of beer, which are lukewarm since the icebox is now full of fish that we have caught along the way. We are standing on the hatchway together and quickly drinking to warm up for the social occasion. I seem to sense a slightly tense, suppressed nervousness among the group; just like before a prom. But we thoroughly enjoy the evening. For the first time in days, the sky has cleared up. The night sky is as luscious as ever and later reveals a bright half moon. The bay lies enchanted in the night, still and silver.

The celebration remains unforgettable. When the bow of the longboat grinds onto the sand the entire population of Susui is already completely assembled on the beach, adorned with fresh flower wreaths. We too receive garlands. Together we move to the meeting house. Once there, we are given our places on the straw mats for the ceremonial welcoming according to a strict hierarchy. The guest from Europe may not turn down the seat of honour. Outside, the children are pressing their faces up against the windows to catch a glimpse. In a giant carved wooden bowl called the *tanoa* the *jaqona* is prepared with ceremonial etiquette.

It is a holy beverage made from water and the pulverised roots of a pepper bush, that must be present at every family celebration, laying of a foundation stone or state occasion across the entire Pacific. The bland, slightly bitter and sedating drink is also served all around with strict etiquette in half coconut shells. We hand over our guest presents of five cartons of cigarettes, a sack of rice, and a half-sack of sugar which we are thanked for both verbosely and ceremonially. Then the atmosphere relaxes as the official part is now over.

Later, after an opulent dinner – ragout of giant clams, goat curry, chicken in *lolo*, fish in *lolo*, taro, cassava and banana pudding – after the graceful synchronised seated dances of the women and the wild, dynamic dances of the men, the real fun begins. It is what we, the tough guys from the *Ai Sokula* have been waiting for, have been fearful of: it is the *Taralala*, the bop, that mild Pacific spoof adaptation of European ballroom dancing. Here, however, the women ask the men to dance: ladies choice all around! We have a lot of fun. Only Bola remains melancholically seated at the edge, firmly defying any advances.

Later that evening, when Patemo has disappeared for a meeting with the village elders, we find out the real reason for the celebration: three-quarters of a year ago, the Chief of Susui died. It is therefore necessary to find a successor. Usually this falls on the oldest son in line to the throne – or like in this case – the oldest son of the Chief's brother. This person is Patemo, merchant captain in Wong's Shipping Company, one of the best navigators in Fijian waters. ('He knows every single reef by heart, even when drunk', says Nathanieli.) It will no doubt be an incisive career change, should Pat decide to accept the offer. A Fijian Chief is a mixture between a village mayor and an absolute ruler, on one hand a government representative and on the other a keeper of the 'heathen', i.e. precolonial, traditions. Either way it is a full time job. Patemo seems very withdrawn when we head back to the *Ai Sokula*.

Our last day. The freighter plods cumbersomely along through the choppy sea beneath rattling gusts of rain. We are heading straight back across the Koro Sea to our home port of Suva. The ship is lying deep

89

in the water, cloaked in the intensive scent combination of coconut oil and diesel. The cargo holds are full of copra sacks, the decks stacked high with empty gasoline barrels. One mile before the reef, the dolphins come to greet us. Cheerful, energetic, elegant. It is a school of ten, maybe fifteen animals that position themselves ahead of the bow of the *Ai Sokula* and guide the old lady through the passage into the Harbour Bay. Captain Patemo says: 'Dolphins are a good omen. Always. I missed them when we took off. Now they are here. That is good.' He sighs, as if he has just been released of something, and raises his eyebrows.

Bola takes me to one side to tell me of his great plan: he asks if we can go to the photographer on Suva and have our picture taken together. He then wants me to send the picture to Losalini with a letter that I will write for him saying that the photo was a present from him and that he was still thinking of her and hoping to see her again soon. Most importantly I need to make clear that he is waiting for a response. It would be impossible for him to write the letter himself. That would be far too direct and not customary in these parts. A South Sea romance! And I am to be the go-between – how wonderful!

The last day, the last hour. Ahead of us lies the wide staggered panorama of mountain tops, hills and valleys surrounding Suva Bay, the mainland, home. Above it are low banks of cloud, dragging leaden grey trails of rain across the green land. The setting sun can only force its intense bundle of glowing orange rays in between momentarily. We pack up our personal effects and prepare to move out. The mood among us is strangely limp; changing between a confident mission-successfully-accomplished feeling and a dampened anticipation of the free days ahead.

Of course we are happy to leave behind the meagre and increasingly bland ship cuisine, are excited about the many possibilities in the city and look forward to finally seeing new faces. But on the other hand? There was something there. Something that just felt right. Who knows if the next trip will be as rounded as the last? Something has come to an end. Particularly for me.

Our farewell drink in the Public Bar in the port ends up being orgiastic since Fijian custom requires everyone to buy one round. And that's just to begin with. We are twelve people. Fortunately I still manage to find my kit bag the next morning.

A Message in a Bottle from Alessandro Malaspina

A Tongan Adventure

The scene must have repeated itself many times in exactly the same or a similar manner during that time, in those expanses: a small group of officers standing on the wide beach of a tropical island in gold-trimmed uniforms, knee breeches and buckled shoes, a detachment of marines with presented arms, ready for anything. Behind them a chaotic mix of sailors and at a befitting distance, a large but tightly huddled group of islanders spellbound by a mixture of mistrust, admiration, bafflement and exhilaration. The first row is taken up by the nobility, the priests and the prince. Grass skirts, spears, war clubs, flower necklaces, feather crowns …

All are gathered around a flagpole that has been rammed into the white sand of the beach, at the top of which – depending on circumstance – a British, French, Dutch, Portuguese or Spanish flag is flapping in the trade wind. A volley is fired, a speech by the commandant, singing of the national anthem, prayer, three cheers for the respective sovereign and finally the ceremonial burying of a charter.

Once again, the appropriation of an 'undiscovered' and therefore according to Eurocentric thinking an 'ownerless' island is completed as part of the competition between the great European powers over colonies and other spheres of influence. The by-product of such an act is that an unassuming island population is lifted out of facelessness and suddenly made subjects of His Majesty George III or Louis XV; transformed without its inhabitants being any the wiser. The only thing they can assume is that their strange visitors' theatrical ceremony usually implies the beginning of the end for them; the beginning of the downfall of their culture, their way of life, their seclusion and their physical and psychological integrity.

Change of scene. Time: 200 years later. Place: a stone mushroom poking straight out of the depths of the sea. The tip of this tiny rocky isle a few metres off the shore of the island of Vava'u provides the setting. And what a remarkable place it is. To one side the white sand is seamed by coconut palms whose crowns are flapping in the trade wind, behind it the seep mountains rise through the impenetrable green wall of the rain forest. On the other side the deep blue sea is endless. Sum total: 100 per cent Pacific panorama, pure and without any western additives.

The six figures on the summit of said picturesque hump of rock are unaware of these beautiful surroundings. Kneeling and squatting in between gnarled bushes they are hacking and digging in the cracks and crevices of the ancient coral rock formation: two Tongans, four Papalangi, all of whom are no longer entirely sane.

One of them is me. If I look up from the hole from which I am shovelling bits of rotten wood, leaves, bird droppings and stones with a small red children's spade, only to wipe the sweat from my brow and briefly stretch my aching back. The Pacific panorama is of little interest to me or my hectically digging neighbours. We are now only concerned with the buried bottle containing the certificate of Alessandro Malaspina. The 200-year-old Spanish bottle. In order to search for it we have clambered and groaned our way to the top of this needle-like tower of porous rock; in order find it we have become maniacs. The fever has grabbed hold of us. Carter must have felt similarly in front of Tutankhamun's tomb.

Just a few hours ago – when we embarked on our amateur archaeological excursion – we had joked about the possibility of a private ceremonial handover of our historical finds to His Tongan Majesty King Taufa'ahau Tupou IV and leaving his residence decorated with medals. Yes, we would have found that particularly comic.

There has been nothing comic about what we are doing since we arrived at the site of the dig. Now we are rummaging doggedly through the holes of this heat releasing lump, dirty and sweaty with just one goal: to find the dreaded bottle.

Of course it is a total failure. What else? We end our search at sunset. Much like the king himself, who dug here years ago, or rather, when taking into consideration his corpulent build, let other people dig. Much like the king at that time we also climb back into the boat with the unsatisfied feeling in mind that if we had only kept going for half an hour longer … The historically documented event simply must have take place here, since the sources are reliable and precise.

The most disappointed among us is Kathleen, the young Australian archaeologist working on Tonga's history who talked us all into going on this crazy excursion. She told us laymen the astonishing story of Alessandro Malaspina and the appearance of the island group Vava'u on charts of the Pacific.

Like Columbus, Malaspina (1754–1809) was an Italian who sailed under the Spanish flag by appointment of the Crown and was similarly poorly rewarded for his services. After becoming the victim of a court intrigue he found himself in prison and was banned from publishing the account of his expedition. As a result he remained the great unknown among the circumnavigating explorers and researchers in the tailwind of the Enlightenment despite now being ranked next to Cook and Lapérouse in his importance to the discovery and mapping of the Pacific.

In the race for trading bases, colonies and areas of influence in the enormous and largely uncharted Pacific basin Spain too wanted its share of the loot. Both France's (Bougainville and Lapérouse) and Britain's (Wallis and Cook) research work made Spain nervous. In order to continue with the unobstructed exploitation of its Philippine territories Madrid required an unhindered sea passage between Manila and Mexico (and across the Atlantic from there). The Spanish had considered the Pacific their domain since the middle of the 16th century and referred to it as the *lago español*. The discoveries made by Balboa, Magellan and their countless successors, the central American colonies and their dominance of trade with the Spice Islands (the Moluccas) justified this claim. But this influence was already dwindling, particularly once France and England began pushing into the Pacific. Now they had to pit themselves against the others.

In those days it meant organising scientific expeditions which required a good deal of patience. It could take up to three years for a flotilla to return home, ideally with a few dominions or perhaps even some profitable colonies in tow. It goes without saying that scientific findings were always abundant: news of glowing volcanoes, giant birds that couldn't fly, descriptions of colossal stone heads that looked out onto the sea with empty eyes, tattooed islanders who didn't know what sin was ...

When Malaspina set off from Cadiz with his two ships *Descubierta* and *Atrevida* in August 1789, the chances of finding any undiscovered Pacific islands or archipelagos was already minimal. It had also been certified and proven that the legendary 'Terra Australis' (not to be confused with Australia) which had been doggedly searched for by James Cook and many others for over 300 years did not exist. The majority of Polynesia, Melanesia and Micronesia had also already been 'discovered' at this stage. Consequently,

Malaspina's voyage was predominantly about making exact maps and compiling detailed ethnographic, geological, biological and nautical reports and finally to make cost-benefit-analyses of colonial engagements.

Malaspina had a comprehensive list of tasks on his agenda: Peru, Hawaii, Alaska (in search of the straits into Hudson Bay), the Philippines, the Galapagos Islands (which were then charted for the first time in detail) and finally the Tongan Vava'u Islands, where he arrived with his well-equipped team of researchers in 1793. However, Malaspina could not claim any fame for the discovery of these islands.

The Spanish explorer was, in fact, best known for his euphoric reports on the beauty of the landscapes, the friendliness of the inhabitants and most of all on the ideal anchoring possibilities, the abundance of fresh water and the fertility of the islands. These factors were what had prompted Spain to send Malaspina out to have a closer look at the treasure that had so unexpectedly fallen into the lap of this most Catholic country.

In truth, Vava'u had been discovered by the young Don Francisco Mourelle twelve years earlier through more of a coincidence than a systematic search for new land. Mourelle had been contracted to sail the frigate *Princessa* which was laden with valuable goods for the Spanish viceroy from Manila to Mexico as quickly as possible. The *Princessa* did not do her name any justice. She was more of a decrepit old lady in desperate need of a rejuvenation treatment and certainly not suited to a timed race across the Pacific. After limping past the Caroline Islands and the Solomon Islands, however, her captain soon discovered that not only the state of the ship, but also her provisions were miserable: legions of cockroaches were destroying the ship's biscuit before the crew's eyes, the salt meat was full of maggots and the water, stored in old barrels, smelt rotten. An island where they could restock needed to be found quickly unless they all wanted the trip to end fatally.

Mourelle was in luck and found an island. On 28 February 1781 the *Princessa* dropped anchor off the coast of Vava'u. Here, he found more than enough water, fruit and pigs. Being the first to set foot on the island, he also found his way into the history books. But Mourelle did not have the time to explore the island. The necessary repairs and restocking of water and food were done in feverish haste. An indication of exactly how much time pressure he was under is the astonishing fact that he forgot to formally claim the island for Spain. This was then made up for, twelve years later, by Malaspina with all the suitable ceremonial effort described earlier.

He did not complete this task without scruples. Malaspina was an educated man of strong classical values and standards. He respected and treated the Tongans as equals, affording them the same rights as himself – a stance which was not commonplace among the Rousseau-influenced explorers of the late 18th century. Yes, he even questioned the moral justification of appropriating such a well-organised and admirably ruled community as Vava'u was at the time of his visit.

But moral scruples and royal orders are two different things. The certificate for the appropriation of the island was buried in a sealed bottle on a tiny rocky island off the coast with all the pomp befitting such an act. Vava'u had become Spanish. According to Malaspina's log book, the document of annexation read as follows: 'His Catholic Majesty's corvettes *Descubierta* and *Atrevida*, under the command of his captains Don Alessandro Malaspina and Don Jose Bustamente y Guerra anchored in this port in May of 1793. After exploring the archipelago all around Vava'u, they took possession of it in the name of His Majesty by hoisting the flag at the observatory point and accompanying this ceremonial act by shouting "Long live the King" seven times.'

Led by their ruler and instructed by their Spanish 'friends', the inhabitants of the island group newly christened Martin-de-Mavorga Islands (after the Spanish viceroy of Mexico) responded with the call '*Vavao foxa España*!' ('Vava'u, son of Spain!'). Did they have any concept of what they were shouting into the sky with such ardour?

Fortunately for the inhabitants of Vava'u this ceremony was the first and last official act of their self-proclaimed masters. (Unfortunately for most other Pacific island populations Vava'u was a singular exception.) The masters never returned. The Tongans have Napoleon to thank for this since the turbulence in Europe at the beginning of the new century allowed Spain to forget all about the small group of islands in the distant Pacific.

But what had Malaspina found when, sailing in the tracks of Mourelle, he first saw the green hills of Vava'u on the horizon?

It was the most diverse, picturesque and beautiful island of the Tonga group. I know of no one who has had the good fortune to travel the entire archipelago who will disagree with this statement. The chain of 169 Tongan islands stretches 300 kilometres from south to north. Only forty-five of these are inhabited and they are structured into four island groups with the densely populated main island Tongatapu which includes the capital of Nuku'alofa located in the south. The panorama consists partly of flat coral islands with far reaching sand beaches, partly of wide spread rock plateaux under which fantastic caves open up, and partly of flawless round volcanoes that grow out of the black depths of the sea in the uninhabited distance.

Vava'u is an absolute 'must see' for trans-Pacific sailors. In addition to all her beautiful landscapes, the island also offers one of the most spectacular and hurricane-safe ports in the Pacific. The entrance itself is already a grand experience: if in luck, one may be guided in by the school of dolphins that has been living here for dolphin generations and is a firmly established element in local mythology. The ship will glide through a winding fjord-like bay for 11 kilometres, past palm-lined villages, jutting cliffs, the mighty table mountain named Mount Talo and countless tiny velvety green overgrown rock islands. Finally the circular bay of turquoise water where yachts from a myriad of countries are floating will open up under the city outline of Neiafu with the white glowing mission church poised on the terraced hillside. Mourelle christened this maritime haven *Puerto de Refugio* and it is still named Port of Refuge today.

As if the dozy charm of a Pacific town in which it seems like the clocks were stopped at the beginning of the century, with its overgrown cliffs, surrounding beach-rimmed islands and mini-islands, its clear coves and shining coral reefs weren't enough, Vava'u also offers the romantic and sporty visitor one more adventure of ancient origin.

The sporty part comes first: near Nuapapu, one of the small islands off shore, where the cliffs break off 10 metres under water, the swell is raising and lowering a boat that is tacked right next to the rocks. A few daring individuals jump overboard equipped with snorkels, masks and flippers. They take a few long breaths, dive underwater and disappear. The boatman is ready for a long wait.

Our diving party has gone 4 metres underwater to a black hole opening in the rock face. We switch our lights on and swim 5 metres straight ahead into the darkness. With our last breath we make it to the surface and arrive in a large cave. The beams of our lamps touch on fantastic arches, every drop unleashes resounding echoes and the surface of the water is glowing jade green from the distant sunshine seeping in through the undersea tunnel. The most incredible part: the cave is alive, it is breathing. At regular intervals of a few seconds, the air inside clouds into thick fog and just as quickly and mysteriously clears again. This continues in a constant eternal rhythm.

Physically this all makes sense: the air in the cave being oversaturated with moisture – the swell of the ocean being pressed in and sucked out – excess pressure followed by a vacuum … and yet, the phenomenon remains a magical experience. I sit on a small rock ledge by the water and feel like I am inside the lungs of an ancient leviathan. Call me Jonah …

And now for the romantic part: about 250 years ago Tonga was once again rocked by violent territorial wars between rival princes. In the middle of this Romeo meets Juliet. But even the Tongan Montagues and Capulets belong to adversarial houses. The water is much too deep for an escape. But not for Romeo. While fishing, he has discovered a cave with a heart-shaped underwater entrance. He brings his Juliet there to keep her safe. They wait in the cave for weeks until the feud has settled down. Then they escape to nearby Fiji and if they were lucky lived happily ever after. This is a story that is loved by Tongans and which they never tire of telling in the evenings when the sun has set and everyone is gathered under the breadfruit trees.

The romantic-maritime cave is called Mariner's Cave because the first Westerner to have discovered and described it was the English sailor William Mariner, who, in the early years, spent four years living on Tonga as the prince's adopted son, the only white man among the 'savages', the only man spared during the massacre of the crew of the English *Port-au-Prince*. Another Tongan tale that could be told ... It took place in 1806, only thirteen years after Alessandro Malaspina's appropriation of Vava'u which fortunately had no adverse consequences for the Tongans. And with that we will leave out many tales of ghosts and beachcombers, English missionaries and Tongan warriors and return to the Spanish bottle. The King never found it and neither did we. In any case, the claim of ownership which it documents has long since expired.

Perhaps it is still resting where it was buried. Perhaps the islanders dug it up as soon as the white sails of the strange visitors disappeared over the horizon. Or perhaps the roots of the trees, the ever-crashing waves and the hurricanes rapidly destroyed this fragile Western legacy. Because it is so unimportant, particularly here, in the endless expanses of the Pacific, when someone says: This place belongs exclusively to us, forever!

The Flight to Tofua
The slow approach to a remote island

Stage 1: Biographical Note

'And now for my Volga-towboat-number! It works every time', Peter says as he turns off the motor, jumps overboard, grabs the ropes and pulls the speedboat and its passengers through the shallows of the lagoon. This is how I first met him twelve years ago in the magic garden island labyrinth of Vava'u, Tonga's most northern island group. 'Quite a character' is the phrase that is used around here to describe him and it is meant with respect and fondness. He is someone who stands out from the rest, who keeps to himself and who looks very closely, one who does his own thing, calm, competent, headstrong. Someone who leaves an impression. Peter Goldstern, in his mid-fifties, gaunt, in top condition, with weathered skin, looks like a mountain guide. And just to break the stereotype, he is also a citizen of New Zealand who grew up in the United States, has both a B.Sc. and an M.Sc. in engineering, is a licensed PADI-Instructor etc. He is also the son of Austrian Jews, which would technically make him an emigrant. His father survived Dachau and Buchenwald so as a German it wasn't all that easy for me to really get to know him.

Last but not least: Peter Goldstern is a passionate and experienced pilot, with no less than 7,000 hours flying time under his belt. As a 'delivery pilot' he flew over 100 single and twin-engine aircraft to Europe, Australia and the South Pacific, sometimes with a cabin full of spare tanks, flying for over twenty hours in one stretch. Always on his own, of course, always arriving safely at his destination. Except for once: 'In December 1979, when I was half-way to Europe, the engine decided to give up and I had to land on the water. That was it. I managed to make an emergency call stating my coordinates and eventually the Canadian Air Force dropped a life raft down to me. A few hours later, a Soviet weather ship fished me out of the water. The only irritating thing about all of this was that this took place just as the conflict in Afghanistan were beginning and for weeks no one would let a Russian ship into port to drop me off.'

On one of his flights across the Pacific Peter Goldstern picked Vava'u as a stopover between Hawaii and Australia. For the very first time a seaplane landed in the still crater lake of the remote, uninhabited volcanic island of Tofua. In that very moment a long-lasting Tongan love affair was born: Peter has been living on Vava'u since 1982. Here, he has found his niche; a small amount of tourism (particularly from New Zealand and Australia) had established itself but there was a lack of any organised sightseeing. So the experienced diver bought equipment and motorboats and founded the company Vava'u Water Sports and began showing visitors the beautiful over and underwater sites of the islands. And if necessary this included his Volga-towboat-number. His dream was to one day own his own seaplane. He has had one since 1992. So he flies to Tofua – with or without passengers.

Stage 2: Historical reminiscence

Everyone recognises the scene and knows the actors: one last hate-filled, unforgiving exchange of glances and Charles Laughton/Trevor Howard climbs down the rope ladder into the dinghy while Clark Gable/Marlon Brando looks on with a stony expression on his face. 'We will see each other again, Mr. Christian!' Captain Bligh calls from below, shaking his fist; while up on deck the mutineers shout 'Off to Tahiti!' This is the famous mutiny on the *Bounty*. Myth, film history and, astonishingly, also historical fact. These events took place in Tongan waters on the morning of 28 April 1789.

Within sight of these events, approximately ten nautical miles north-east, an island looms on the horizon. From it a white cloud is rising into the sky like a billowing sail. Bligh is steering toward the island 'where a volcano almost always burns on the highest peak', in the hope of restocking his dwindling water and food reserves. The island and its inhabitants receive the sailors inhospitably: a storm is brewing, there is no good anchoring ground to be found, fruit and fresh water are rare and the islanders' curiosity switches to animosity as soon as they realise that the travellers have not brought gifts or goods for trade. With the exception of quartermaster John Norton, who is knocked down by the hail of rocks thrown at them by their attackers, everyone scrambles back to the boat in time and manages to row away in desperation.

Here is where one of the greatest nautical achievements begins – and it must be mentioned even if it is not really relevant at this point: the voyage of William Bligh and his seventeen crewmembers to Timor, 6,500 nautical miles in a dangerously overloaded open boat, through storms, periods of dead calm and reefs, without charts and a minimal amount of water and food. They could have had both in large quantities if they hadn't been refused access to the ring-shaped mountain of that seemingly inhospitable island. They would have been able to see flocks of wild ducks happily quacking and paddling in the enormous freshwater reservoir of the Crater Lake lying beneath the cosily smoking volcano. They would have discovered Tofua's inner paradise, girded by mountains, deeply hidden from the outside world.

Stage 3. Vulcanological digression

Tonga's imposing King Taufa'ahau Tupou IV reigns over about 170 islands. Approximately. The number changes because some islands are of temporary nature. Occasionally a new one will appear only to disappear again after a few years or decades or even stay ...

There are many other things that also fluctuate in this area. After all, this Polynesian island kingdom in the south-western Pacific is located directly in one of the most geophysically active zones on earth and essentially owes its existence to this activity. One hundred nautical miles east, one of the most cavernous deep sea trenches runs parallel to the Tonga group of islands. It is called the Tonga and Kermadec Trench, which forms part of the 'Ring of Fire' and measures up to 10,000 metres in depth. It is the place where the Pacific Plate is pushed under the Indo-Australian Plate and the parts of it are recycled in the melting pot under the earth's crust. Huge amounts of energy are released along these subduction zones which manifest themselves as volcanic and seismic activity.

When the plates rattle in the kitchens across Tonga, the locals are not at all bothered by such events because it is part of everyday life. But not quite so everyday is the appearance of new islands on the national map. And yet it does happen ever so often. Some are familiar because they come and go, like Falcon Island, which has appeared and disappeared half a dozen times in the last hundred years. The former happens abruptly with lots of noise and the latter happens on the quiet, bit by bit. The same happened with Late'iki, which is located 40 nautical miles from Tofua. The last time it broke through the water surface hissing and glowing in 1979, His Majesty christened it and the Crown Prince ceremoniously claimed it by planting the national flag on it. Within a few years, however, waves, wind and storms carried away the loose layers of volcanic rock, ash and lava that made up this new land. But the chimney of the volcano that grew out of the depths until just below the surface of the ocean was merely sleeping. This year in June it awoke and cleared its throat rather deafeningly. For many nights the inhabitants of nearby islands could see a red glow on the horizon which turned into an immobile cloud that stood on the separating line between sea and sky like a white bulb. That's what we had come to see: a South Sea island *in statu nascendi*.

Stage 4: Airborne Action

At eight in the morning Peter arrives at the airstrip of Lifuka from Vava'u. Lifuka is on the main island of the Ha'apai group located in the middle of Tonga — let's not get into more detail than that. We sign the agreement entitled 'Dear Customer' which explains that we are responsible for ourselves and shouldn't touch anything on board the aircraft. I squeeze myself into the co-pilot seat, Gisela takes the tiny remaining space behind it, the Perspex door is clicked shut, we roll onto the runway, prepare for take off and after a short sprint we smoothly lift off above the palm trees, huts, turquoise-jade-green lagoon and the grey-brown wall of the reef, against which the constant waving azure of the Pacific rolls on for kilometres. Just as professionally as on a Boeing, the landing gear is retracted and we are airborne. I love the term 'airborne'. Just as it suggests, we are carried by the air heading west, slowly and right above the rippling waves, the wide breathing swell of the Pacific Ocean. Gisela nudges me from behind and points down: we can follow the trail of the whales heading north along the coast.

Time passes differently when flying. It certainly doesn't fly, it stops, accumulates, turns into dreaming or unspecific staring, it passes unused and doesn't count, isn't real time. Forty minutes: was it long? Short? There is nothing outside that the eye can attach itself to. Then, finally, we spot a thick milky-white cloud far in the distance growing out of the sea on the endless horizontal line of silver and grey. Soon after, a dark, crannied, steaming lump that looks like a burnt loaf of bread materialises beneath it, looking barren and empty. The crater at its centre contains a red glow. The ocean surrounding it breaks on the coast with hiss and sulphur green and yellow streaks spread into the distance for kilometres. We circle above it all like a small moth, breathless. So this is how the earth is created. It is a sunny day in August, any day for that matter, but it is also a day of creation.

This eruptive island baby is only a few weeks old, measuring 40 metres in height and several hectares of surface. When it was born, the volcano shut itself up by forming a thick plug of baked lava on the top of its fiery abyss. But underneath this protective layer, the lava continues to bubble. According to experts, it is not unlikely that a highly powerful eruption will occur once the pressure inside blows off the volcano lid. In the meantime, the government has declared the area within a 10-mile radius of the island a no-go zone after a Tongan marine patrol discovered that the steaming salt water forms hydrochloric acid when mixed with volcanic gases.

We head south towards Tofua. But first we circle

Kao, Tofua's beautiful sister island. Peter points towards it and says: 'Look there, the Queen'. A cone fit for a geometry textbook emerges from the mist. It simply is the perfect form of a mountain, a vision; the flawlessly rounded, velvety green volcano is poised on the surface of the blue sea with a bright white flag of smoke raised at its peak. At 1,100 metres, it is Tonga's highest peak: extinguished, uninhabited, distant and unapproachable. In a gallery of the most beautiful mountains on earth, Kao could not be left out and would easily hold its own next to Mount Fuji and Mount Kilimanjaro.

Stage 5. Shangri-La Pacifica

Tofua cannot compete with Kao in appearance because although it is three times the size of Kao, its tip has been flattened by an eruption many centuries ago. Peter Goldstern pulls the plane 500 metres up to the edge of the mountain's circular edge. We are surprised by something of a miracle: as if two films that have nothing to with each other had been played right after another without any sign of interruption.

What was the familiar South Sea panorama of rolling dunes, reefs, lagoons and an endless palette of opalescent colours has suddenly turned into a landscape reminiscent of Canada, the Eifel or Bavarian mountain lakes ... I can see deep forests, chains of hills, a large, still, freshwater lake untouched by even the slightest breath of wind. The aircraft takes a dip toward the glassy surface and suddenly turns from a plane into a speedboat. The water splashes up against the fuselage right under our feet, waves froth up against the cabin window and we head toward the shore at high speed.

Silence surrounds us and is only deepened by bird calls in the distance. We observe quietly – and are infatuated by the knowledge that we are the only humans in this faraway world surrounded by mountains and the ocean. Shangri-La Pacifica. Peter lets his guests enjoy these first breathless minutes of overwhelming emotion whilst he moors his aircraft in the shallows.

Far from the opposite lakefront, about half way between the shore and the bordering crater ring, a small active volcano steams away relentlessly. That is where we want to go. We fetch kayaks from the base camp which Peter has set up with a large tent with camp beds and an open fire and paddle across the water. Again, the association that springs to mind is Canada; all we are missing to complete this picture are some bears, Indians and trappers.

Although I previously described the volcano as 'small', I think I would use a different adjective at this very moment. We have already been climbing toward its peak for an hour. First we went through thick bush – feathery casuarinas, scaly fern trees, pale violet panicles, curious kingfishers hopping from branch to branch at arm's length from us – then we crossed a steep ash rockpile. Every stone we dislodge with our feet tumbles endlessly into the depths so we have to make sure not to trip without any decent hiking shoes on. Down below the plane is resting on the water like a small pond insect. Like a mouth wide open in a scream toward the sky, the edge of the crater rises out of the black lunar landscape. We lean over the sulphurous, steaming edge carefully, but cannot see the bottom. Glowing lumps shoot out of the darkness, but not far enough to reach us. Peter points out that, like the lake, the volcano is probably around 200 metres deep. He adds that the last big 'bang' was many decades ago, but the rumbling coming from the depths is impressive and the surface of this newborn volcano is too fresh for us to feel like we are on safe ground. The earth's surface is being baked in a spot like this; it always has and always will. We are as small as ants: superfluous and out of place. We decide it is time to leave.

Peter slowly gains altitude by flying in large circles until we can surmount the 500-metre circular wall protecting the inner lake. We enjoy long panoramic farewell images of a lonely and magical world. They will no doubt stay with us forever. We fly over the rim of the enclosure and return to the South Seas. Foaming white surf, atolls, reefs and endless ocean. Before we leave Tofua's rugged coastline behind Peter points down and exclaims: 'Look there, Bligh's landing place!' We see a small indentation, barely large enough to be a cove, and a hint of a cave in the cliffs along the rocky beach. Somewhere in those woods, the unlucky quartermaster John Norton's grave is hidden. The islanders buried him next to one of their warriors after their battle with Bligh and his men so that he would prevent ghosts of the white men from roaming the island ...

How the Pigs once Stole Michael York's Show

Christmas on Rarotonga/Cook Islands

In December, Rarotonga receives its guests in the noblest manner. The flame trees along the coastal road are in full bloom and the obligatory brief downpours of the hurricane season beat down a large amount of their magnificent scarlet leaves onto the asphalt every day. As a result, the entire island is covered with a bright red carpet which visitors from the cool northern zones take as an omen of the much praised hospitality of the Polynesians. They certainly won't be disappointed.

Even the customs officer at the small airport is more interested in whether the visitor has comfortable quarters to stay in and with whom he is celebrating Christmas than in his luggage. And then there is the jolly Maori family who have lined up to greet a relative but also welcome a somewhat confused Papalangi with a beaming *'Kia Orana!'* and scented flower wreaths as though they had been waiting for him.

'Kia Orana!' This greeting will be heard and responded to all day long from now on – sincerely and with a smile. *'Kia Orana!'* May you live! Or: To your wellbeing! How could one possibly be unwell in the summer warm, delightfully blossoming island garden? One thing is certain; this tropical atmosphere does not prompt any Christmassy sentiments. Against the backdrop of the jade green lagoon and white sails of the outriggers the silver-bearded cardboard Santas, glittering plastic fir trees and jingle-bells-music on the waterfront of Avarua seem strange and most certainly out of place.

In the bungalow of the telecommunication department which is located next to an impressive satellite dish which towers over the palm trees I hear a distant crackling voice from Germany telling me about freezing rain, mulled wine and Christmas tree decorating. Operator Tutakimoa asks me what the news from my island is. I tell him that it is cold and people are wearing wool socks and jumpers. Tutakimoa shake himself and exclaims: 'Poor folks over there!' It is very hot and we decide to head for a swim.

How do the Cook Islanders celebrate Christmas? I am told that the 24th is movie day. But first we take the somewhat clumsy outrigger along the reef to Taatoka Island to collect palm fronds and casuarina branches to wear as festive accessories and as a substitute for a fir tree. We paddle the boat through the crystal clear water on our knees while under us the rainbow bright magical coral garden grows. On my right, the surf is swelling over the reef like a green glass wall, seemingly all consuming but essentially powerless despite its impressive thundering and white explosive spray. On my left the vegetation forms a lush expanse to frame the theatrical backdrop of jagged volcanic rocks.

I stroll down the main road with Teariki and Sarah, the owners of the little guest lodge on the beach, with grandparents and a horde of children, past the seat of government which consists of a two-storey wooden house with a few reserved parking bays for designated officials; Premier – Minister of Agriculture & Marine & Scientific & Industrial Research – Minister of Post and Telecommunications. There are no barriers, no secure zone around the building, no federal guards, nothing. Half the city is on foot, everyone knows everyone, laughter and *'Kia Orana'* from all directions. Even Mr Premier and his family are on their way to the cinema with a *'Kia Orana'*.

The Empire Theatre (no doubt which empire is meant) is a white-painted wooden auditorium built in the typically tropical colonial gingerbread style. This includes the most beautiful and opulent cast-iron green velvet covered seats dating back to imperial silent film days. There isn't a single seat left empty on this afternoon. Appropriately for the time of year, we watch Zeffirelli's big-screen adaptation of the life of Jesus Christ. Outside the open side doors the tops of the palm trees are rustling in the sea breeze while somewhere close by a brook is drip dropping toward the sea over volcanic rocks and chickens are clucking on the lawn.

The great old story being played on the screen is grandiloquent and colourful and everyone is commenting on what is happening at any given moment – be that from a Methodist, Catholic, Mormon or an Adventist point of view. Pontius Pilate (Rod Steiger) would not have a very good time on Rarotonga but Mary Magdalene (Anne Bancroft) has won the favour of all. We end up crying a lot.

When the fur-clad John the Baptist (Michael York) launches into his blazing penitential sermon, he has lost the audience's attention. Somehow a pack of dogs decided to wake the pigs dozing on the muddy banks of the river and loudly chase the protesting creatures into the cinema full of reverent spectators. There is a great deal of barking, squeaking, cheering, screaming, a wild chase and a lot of fun. Michael York's efforts are futile.

Was it sloppiness or perhaps clever dramatic premeditation that made the projection assistant play the first reel last and leave the viewers with festive images of the manger in Bethlehem as they walked home in the sunset? As on every other evening, the indescribable colour spectacle gilding the sky outdoes any Technicolor or Cinemascope qualities and leaves the sky, land and sea dipped in gold. Over the peaks of Rua Manga, dark mountains of clouds are forming and producing wild flashes of light. A rumbling sound announces the next thunderstorm. Nature gives us its own version of Son et Lumière.

Where does one head after the cinema for one (or maybe a few) drinks? There is really no question, mainly because of a lack of alternatives: we aim for the Banana Court, which has been an institution on the island for decades and is well known across the Pacific. As the saying goes, 'You haven't been in Raro if you haven't been at BC'. Banana Court is where all of Rarotonga meets; it is a discotheque, a singing school, parliamentary lobby, gossip exchange, local hang-out and kissing corner for lovers. The band plays sentimental Polynesian tunes, sweetened the Hawaiian way, ceiling fans stir uselessly through the overwhelming scent cocktail of coconut oil, rum and flower wreaths. It is tightly packed around the bars and the dance floor, which quickly disperses the few tourists there might be.

At the stroke of midnight ('Last orders please!') and with astonishing compliance considering everyone's raised alcohol levels, the party is over. The night gives one last howl as hundreds of scooters and mopeds are started – some worryingly wobbly – and disappear into the darkness. Then we are left only with the eternal voice of the island: the never-ending grumbling of the surf on the reef.

Even those who aren't waiting with baited breath for what Santa Claus has put in their stocking by the fireplace (which should be taken metaphorically since no one in these parts wears stockings, let alone has a fireplace), i.e. those who enjoy sleeping in are woken at first light (and not just on Christmas morning) by the Rarotongan triad: there is the *basso continuo* of the surf, the high pitched barking of dogs and the crowing of countless cockerels. Every paradise has its serpent.

Today the wake-up call comes at the right time: we rise for the morning service in the old mission church of Titikaveka, a solid fortress with metre-thick whitewashed walls. Whether the message proclaimed by the powerfully eloquent pastor in vowel-rich Rarotongan is a happy one remains a mystery to this foreigner. The cloudy expression on the preacher's face and the repeated gloomy chants of 'Amen!' make me somewhat doubtful. But then they begin to sing powerfully and in harmony, in a way that only Polynesians can sing. The melody is familiar: 'Silent night, holy night.' One person sings in German. It is Christmas.

After the service, the congregation stands together chatting among the flower-hung cement blocks of the graveyard and dinner invitations are exchanged. Ultimately, I end up with three. Declining any would be an affront. Teariki decides on the order in which I will attend. The most important thing is to visit the *Ariki*'s home last, since he is the aristocratic leader of the region. Any other sequence would be an insult. Three Polynesian banquets in one night …

The holiday rest is sacred. Even a brief visit to the reef to spear some fish would be against local custom. As a result, I have plenty of time for a long leisurely walk on the *Ara Metua*. It was built over 1,000 years ago as a procession road, a *via sacra polynesiensis*, the oldest preserved road in Oceania, built from coral blocks in the fertile coastal strip that runs along the foot of the mountains. Apples, lemons, papayas, tangerines, oranges, bananas, guavas, mangoes … The overgrown path leads through fruit plantations of paradisiacal fertility. Strewn among them are small bungalows, which look proper and middle class and unmistakably characterised by a Kiwi influence, surrounded by a frenetic flowerage. Hibiscus hedges as high as trees blossom in lemon yellow, salmon red and crimson. It would certainly be a pleasure to be a gardener in these parts.

Guest banquet III involves heroic strength of will. As with meals I and II, the long table is weighed down by pork cooked in an earth oven, with chicken, crayfish, crab and fish – boiled, fried or grilled with vegetables and fruits of all shapes and sizes, presented on whole banana leaves, garnished with flower petals. Friends and relatives from neighbouring islands in the archipelago report on the course of the year: the storms were unprecedented, the turtles they caught were enormous, as were the killer sharks they only barely escaped from ... I learn a lot about the much-joked-about habit of the Cook Islanders to elaborate and exaggerate everyday events into larger-than-life adventures. I had already been warned about this with a smile on Samoa: 'Only believe half of what a Raro-tonga-Maori tells you. And you can be sure it is the wrong half.' But since everyone here knows that the others also know, everything is just fine.

I return home under a sky filled with shooting-stars and spot an irregular chain of spear-fisher torches glittering offshore. Surely they can't be fishing on the holiday? But as I check my watch, I realise that it is ten minutes past midnight and therefore the favourite local sport after bowling is no longer banned by church law. I gather my flashlight and spear and wade through the lagoon to the reef.

December 26th, Boxing Day, is the real highlight of the Christmas holidays on the islands because Boxing Day is also racing day. This means there are horse races on Muri Beach, which – if a greater increase in beauty were a meaningful description – is probably the most beautiful landscape of the island. The lagoon spreads over 800 metres and has three tree-lined islands with white sand beach floating in its waters. The coral labyrinths by the reef are magic gardens of colours and shapes pulsating and glowing with dazzling life.

Slowly the little field shaded by gigantic casuarinas fills with people. The tourists arrive on foot and the prestige-conscious Rarotongans use either motorbikes or pick-ups for even the shortest distances. Small wiry horses, predominantly bred for these races, are bridled and groomed while saddles are frowned upon. The jockeys, who are all boys between ten and fifteen, pin start numbers to their t-shirts. The announcer opens the tote board and begins to animate people to place bets while the trophies are put on display for the audience. All along the racetrack, large families settle for picnics and guitars and ukuleles are tuned. Small children throw sea cucumbers at each other in the shallows of the lagoon. High up in the sky fair-weather clouds sail westwards. A light breeze blows blossom-scented air toward us. Out on the open water, a pod of whales swims along the reef spraying fountains from their blowholes.

The race begins. Like a horde of young Huns the cavalcade breaks loose in a stretched gallop across the sand and through the shallows, all the way to the leaning palm at the tip of the cape and back again. Not all the horses are interested in this much exertion though when faced with a pasture ideal for grazing and waters perfect for bathing. The quitters are rewarded with extra applause, since the audience can understand them all too well. The most important thing, however, is the presentation of prizes since it provides an opportunity for a ceremony. And there isn't really anything the Polynesians enjoy more than a ceremony that is perfect in form. Well there is one thing: laughing together, telling stories, eating, singing, dancing, loving and a sense of community. In other words: having a lovely time. Together. That is the most important thing.

We certainly did have a lovely time. *Kia Orana*, Rarotonga!

Church, Commerce
and Circumstances

Three colonial monologues

For three all-too-short weeks, this traveller lived on an uninhabited island. I did this after receiving head shaking consent from the island owners who could not relate to my strange desire for a Robinson Crusoe-esque escapade.

The urge to occasionally retire into undisturbed privacy is completely foreign to the Polynesians' sense of community. One lives and is embedded in the extended family, tribal hierarchy and village collective – day and night, from birth to death. Anyone who wants to be all alone must be unwell and therefore taken care of.

And now this abstruse request to be left alone on the neighbouring island! Why alone? They are at a complete loss, attempt to talk me out of it, make alternative suggestions ... It was hard and in the end they resigned. 'How could anyone possibly understand these white folk? All of them are slightly neurotic,' they must have thought. So they equipped me, the crazy man from *Yuropin*, with the most opulent provisions, filled me up with good advice, promised to visit me regularly and sailed back across the strait with worried looks on their faces.

It is a tiny island. Two silver-white sand coves, three dark stone cliffs, a chain of hilltops rounded like a cat's back, overgrown with 6-foot high mission grass whispering in the wind, about 100 coconut palms curving their way down the hillside toward the shore, a small stream hidden in the mangrove thicket, the surrounding coral reef in front of which the surf continually plays its *basso continuo* melody. Above it all, an unchanging endless sky.

The hut on the beach is made from branches and leaves, artfully joined but in a makeshift fashion. It is just the beginning of a house and a proposition for a settlement, nothing more. Nonetheless, at an impressive 6 × 4 metres with one door, one window, one bedstead, one table and one stove it is the dominant feature of the bay. The island is alone, belongs to itself. Its landlords from the neighbouring island only come there once every few months to harvest coconuts, cut down trees, catch crabs in the stream and pull taro-tubers out of the swamp. For those few days there is laughter and life around the hut. Afterwards silence returns.

They had warned me about one part of the island. Sheepishly they had avoided any real explanations but had indicated that it might be better to avoid one specific section of the coastline that consisted of a deserted muddle of black lava cliffs and fallen rocks heaped in the shallow waters. Not that anything would happen to me there … but one could not rule the possibility out … certainly not after dark … the place had always been sort of, well … – cursed? – Something like that. – Ghosts? – Yes, ghosts, the undead. One could hear voices there.

How exciting! When I was on my way somewhat delayed after one of my lonely trips across the
island and came past precisely those dark cliffs, the
wind suddenly became fresher. A frosty cool air blew
in from the hills and the white foam surf danced in
the lagoon. Was I mistaken, or were those really the
sounds of whispers, of many hoarse voices floating
in on the cold wind? Nonsense, of course: it was the
rattling leaves of the mangroves and the gurgling of
water between the rocks. What else? Undoubtedly.
I picked up my pace. Better to leave this difficult
terrain and get back to the hut before darkness fell.
The web of panting voices was left behind me:

The Missionary
(Hectic, fast. With a tendency to emphasise single
words without much dramatic logic. Cultivated
upper-class accent which slides into the more common
when she gets angry.)

'Please excuse me Sir for approaching you as a
lady, but you are a white man. European I assume,
Protestant if I am correct? Oh yes I can see it your

eyes, can feel it, in fact. There are so few white people who come here, people one can talk to; one of us, who understands what things are really about. There is so much left to do to complete this work, isn't there? And Rome is not sleeping. They confuse the poor children, those white-habited monks from France. When after all it was us who laid the foundations, switched on the light in their confused souls. It was us who got there first, us! And how far we had already got! They were already wearing civilised clothing, well the women at least and certainly on Sundays. That was all our doing, ours alone! May God be blessed for the day that their dark pagan priests, their wild chieftains came before our house of God and threw their abject idols into the cleansing flames with their own hands. Obscene carved sculptures with enormous – oh if you had seen them! – erect – in all uncovered directness. Monstrous shafts, covered with – oh please spare me the description! – Ornaments of unbelievable ... They had renounced them. With jubilation in their hearts, yes, yes!, they sang the chorales. They really do love to dance those poor children. And to dance!

What a plague it is to drive that dancing out of them! It really was intolerable. Close to the blazing fire, velvet skin, shining with fragrant oils, naked bodies, twitching to the wild rhythm of the drums, stomping feet, trembling bodies, outstretched arms and the luring smile of the tempter – Lord forgive them, for they … cooing laughter in the darkness of the trees, hugs, screams – bodies softly entwined … No, no, no! It really was intolerable. We have managed to expunge that, consistently and with God's help. Not all of them, but most of them, even if hesitantly at first, began to love or at least recognise the value of a God-fearing life of discipline, work and praise of the Lord. And all of this long before the Padres came to steal the fruits of our labours in the name of God, those jealous-eyed papist sneaks! They put themselves behind Chief Maupopapa'o, that dirty little apostate, please excuse my blunt choice of words! They secretly drank wine, those bigoted hypocrites, fornicated with the black women and purported to be servants of God, that sanctimonious pack! They stirred those wogs up against us, secretly gave them weapons

– how false and two-faced. So, undoubtedly, we had to defend ourselves, call upon our fosterlings to help fight against the Antichrist! Their salvation was precious to us, they were entrusted to our care, those poor spiritual children. We had Winchester shotguns and machetes, we were ready! Yes indeed, they hadn't expected that! As the Lord says in Matthew 3:7: You brood of vipers! Who warned you to flee from the coming wrath? They could not outrun it. Twenty-five shotguns! We had trained our boys well. They do have a natural gift for hunting. – Oh so much blood, oh my God!, all those screams and moans! But they died for a just cause. Here, here on this beach, look around you!, here is where the battle was fought, here is where the blood of martyrs flowed and remains as an accusation ever since. This is where we drove the cowardly brood of Marian worshippers into the sea. This is where I too gave my earthly body for the triumph of the London mission on the islands of darkness. I was just reloading Reverend McMurray's second shotgun when the bullet hit me. Since then I have been missing my right eye and my dress is somewhat stained, which I truly regret. Do not pay attention to it, sir! Twenty-eight of the entrusted ones went with me. But what does the Lord say in Revelations 16:6 – For they have shed the blood of saints and prophets, and thou hast given them blood to drink. Oh yes! We let them drink blood, that Roman brood and their ensnared vassals – may the Lord have mercy on their souls! I will have a monument erected, here on this sacred spot where they clubbed Reverend McMurray to death. I still managed to see it. He stared at me, covered in blood, and I stared at him, that divine man, with my remaining eye I steadfastly looked on until the very end, ignoring my pain. And oh my God! In his last moments his dying lips formed the shape of my name: Katherine. Not Sister Katherine, not Miss Hathlethorpe. I …'

The Merchant

(With a distinct Viennese twang, yet frequently and briefly attempting a well-educated and refined accent. He is an ingratiating conversationalist with a put-on *bonhomie*.)

'Pardon me, doctor, if I may, just a wee moment, just a question among fellow countrymen, if I may: The copra, I wanted to know, the copra, where is the copra at today? We never hear anything round here. And mother of pearl? Did it go up then? What was that? Could you possibly give me some information then – totally non-binding of course … Keep it down will you, all you hideous chimeras! All that screaming is so unbearable, I know. You see, I have been trading in copra for twenty years now down on those islands. And now this thing down in Serbia! What's all the talk about Sarajevo? The Crown Prince, you see, I mean did they kill him then or what? But to start a war just because of that, I mean don't we have enough problems already. We have a different perspective down here, don't we? But there is a war over there, right? And how is the copra doing in their markets? I have around twenty-five tonnes altogether at the moment, it's been a good season this year, but only if I can turn it over, only then! But when people start talking about war up there in Europe, then I can't get rid of the stuff. And twenty-five tonnes isn't exactly a small amount and it rots real fast in the wet season. At this rate I might as well tip it all into the lagoon. Why are you running away like that, doc? You mustn't pay attention to the ghosts, that's just how it is round here. What a life! I want to tell you something, I know you'll understand cause I just have an eye for these things – between you and me – you just won't believe it: Fifteen! Fifteen thousand in gold! That's what I made out here in twenty years. A miserable life, all those years among these naked wogs on this damn island. But still: fifteen thousand in gold! And for what, you'll ask. For what? For my very own tobacco store. And where? On the Kärntnerstraße – are you familiar with Vienna? Well it's directly on the corner of Kärntner and Stock im Eisen, opposite Steffl's shop. Now what do you say to that! I have the option, so it's practically mine. International newspapers, tobacco, cigarettes – best clientele all year round. Prime location – nothing can really go wrong. And then they go and kill Franz-Ferdi, those damn anarchist Serbs, and make a huge war out of it all! And I am the one who has to suffer after slaving away all these years among the savages. War and inflation go hand in hand, everybody knows that. I'd almost prefer to stay here, but I've gotta go! You see, doc, they are after me! They are trying to pull me down, those two: Case and old Randall, the drunken pig. They are traders for the competition. And all that bother even though the island would provide enough for both companies and the wogs are essentially all right – stupid, but well-meaning when you know how to handle them. They wouldn't have caused us any trouble. But Case, that rat, he was just too greedy. From the very first day I set foot on this island he was after me. Always trying to provoke me and trying to turn the chiefs against me. You go ahead and do that, I thought, I won't rise to your bait. But then one of their copra sheds burnt down, a really rotten one, with less than four tonnes in it. I mean, why would I do such a thing, if I gain nothing from it but trouble? I'll tell you what I think: Case set it on fire himself. I'm sure it wasn't Randall, he wasn't really good for much anymore – all that gin, you see. But it was that rat Case. He stirred those wogs up real good. Turned them against me so badly that they stuck me in taboo for arson. Do you know what that means? It means no more clients from one day to the next – and not a single kilo of copra either! When at the same time they all had debts with me and the chiefs had the highest of all. I had to defend myself, what else could I have done. It was about my business after all, my tobacco store, my future. And that how it goes, I suppose. I don't want to bore you, really. So anyway it all ended in the shooting on the beach. They say I hit Randall in the stomach, but who knows. Either way, he died three nights later. I'll tell you something though: with him, every bullet was a waste, because he was already so high up on the list, what with his liver and all, a total wreck. And then Case got me. Case and the taboo and the black magic of the wogs. They burnt out my innards while I was still alive. Everything I touched was poisoned. I spent days and nights screaming. Believe you me, I am not the whinging type, no sir, but there was nothing else I could do. I took all the anaesthetic I could find in the medicine box. It was all for nothing, because I was already past it. But please, doctor, please tell me yourself that this doesn't count, I mean it happens every day down here, not to mention the malaria. This can't possibly count, now that I have all my gold together. After all, I'm Austrian, I don't belong among these people. These drivelling spirits, you can hear for yourself, screaming around, I mean where are we! Magic, I'm begging you ...'

The Sailor
(Speaking in slang, with a forced ironic tone that poorly disguises his panic. Is quickly unsettled by the other louder, more eloquent voices.)

'Aloha mister! What brings you to us rattling bones? Did you at least arrive, as one should, with rushing sails, mast-high singing of the oilskins at the anchor capstan and the shrill whistle of the boatswain? Shoot, well obviously not, you come from another time, I can see that. You haven't crossed the line yet either? I have to ask, as I can't know for sure. To tell you the truth: let the rest go, skipper, its better that way, believe me! You familiar with three-masters? Have you ever ridden before the mast? On a whaling ship from Nantucket or New Bedford? No, you haven't. But I'll tell you something: you stand in the bow of the first boat, six oars behind you rowing as hard as they can against the early sun, the fog is lifting, the surf is as dull as a sleepy giant, the ocean is as limp as oil. And then he blows. An old bull, solitary, a hermit, mean and shrewd. You can feel it in your blood. A grandson of old Moby. He knows what's after him. And you cradle the shaft of the harpoon, balance against the water, scream for the rowers to give their all. Then you are poised above the grey mountain. Good god, that enormous whale, he could have crushed us at any moment. He certainly had the head to do it. I often wondered why he hardly ever fought back. I would never have held it against any of them. Did you ever hear about the *Essex*? She was run down by one of them in the end, that has been documented. I was always waiting for something like that to happen. But nothing. They let themselves be slaughtered; they groaned and moaned, rolled over and sprayed their bloody foam over us.

The worst was seeing their eyes when they knew they were going to die. That big dark gleaming eye that asks you, confused, without any anger. And you ram the harpoon into his side again. You push all of your weight into it. Like a spade into the ground. So that it can finally be over. They never defended themselves. And we made candles out of them. That's what they had to die for. Oh well, that eventually ended too. That damn petroleum shit. Well, mister, what can I say? I stayed in these parts. The islands! The islands always had me in their grip. They just are like that. And the girls from the island, well of course. So I decided to stay. Then labour trade came about. Black-birding, selling people. Let's just be honest and call it slavery, because that is what it was. Stealing people, luring them onto boats, those clueless, foolish island wogs who would have strangled their own mothers for an axe blade – they just don't know any better. Manpower for the plantations here and over there. Preferably young men, unmarried, of low social rank. Those were the ones who were easiest to fool, because they wanted to get out and see the world. And if not, booze would always help. Or a good hit to the head, I mean what else was there left to do. It was a solid, establish trade. With fixed contracts and good profits. Forty Solomons for Levuka, hundred to Sava'i and so forth. With a hundred you had to load hundred thirty. Twenty per cent loss was actually considered low. They just died on you during the trip, once they figured out what was going on. They just kicked the bucket. Because they wanted to. How did they do it? They just can. They sit in a corner, stare into space and make themselves go away. It had to get real bad before those niggers finally got rebellious. But when that happened: massacre! You couldn't even load and shoot as quickly as they attacked you. With nails and teeth at your throat. The deck all covered in blood like soft soap. After all, they knew they had nothing left to lose. That's exactly how it was on the old *Emma Bell*. Our last trip. We battled storms for nineteen days with sixty-odd black devils below deck. Until we ran onto the outer reef near Nukapau. That is when they used their chance. Well. The water rushed into the boat and that goddamn brood of heathens launched itself at us. The whole thing was hopeless and lost. The few of us who were left jumped over-board. We didn't even think of putting out the boats. Just down onto the reef, into the swell. Those whose bones weren't crushed by the rocks were drowned like kittens by the Solomons. Would I be here otherwise? I guess I had to pay the price. I wouldn't have changed a thing. It's an occupational hazard. Hey, Skipper, listen, I don't mean to – I just have a few questions. I am on the other side you know. Oh shoot, okay, that's the whole problem – isn't it ...'

A Dream of Paradise
Putting a myth to the test

S lender coconut palms swaying in the gentle Trade
Wind – jade green lagoons bordered by white
sand beaches – the surf forming a wall of spray in
front of the coral reef – crystal clear waterfalls in the
depths of the rainforest – smiling islanders, adorned
with flowers like in a Gauguin painting … the magic
of the South Seas. The acme of all holiday dreams,
praised in travel brochures all across the world. Mel-
lifluous, candy-coloured, sticky-sweet. This gushing
enthusiasm has its own history and its origin can be
pinpointed exactly:

The setting is a dreary autumn evening in an

157

elegant London club during the last decade of the 18th century: outside, brown leaves are whirling from the trees while inside the fireplace and candles are spreading a cosy contemplative atmosphere. In a secluded corner three men are sitting around a table in deep armchairs, drinking claret and smoking whilst engrossed in excited discussion. They are swapping travel anecdotes and memories. The youngest of the group is a German naturalist and author named Georg Forster who accompanied James Cook on his second circumnavigation of the world between 1772 and 1774. He comments:

'The shore, whose snaking curves we followed upwards brought us to a vertical rock face that was draped in many pleasant smelling plants and bushes and from which a crystal-clear column of water tumbled into a small pond whose charming outline paraded all kinds of colourful flowers. It was one of the most beautiful places I have ever seen.'

'How right you are, Monsieur Forster! I travelled to the centre of the island many times and it struck me as a veritable Jardin d'Eden.' Forster's companion

Louis Antoine de Bougainville is 20 years his senior, in his mid-sixties and makes an impressive appearance in his gold-braided admiral's uniform. He too had been one of the very first to circumnavigate the globe between 1765 and 1769. He continues with a smile:

'I saw the most beautiful fields, covered in the most exquisite fruit trees and intersected by small streams, which spread a delicious freshness everywhere. We found groups of men and women camping in the shade of the trees who greeted us amiably. We experienced hospitality, calmness and gentle enjoyment everywhere. Seemingly these people were very happy.'

Now the third in the group begins to talk; William Bligh is also in uniform but his is the far less lavish attire of a lieutenant-commander. Having also been one of Cook's travel companions and commander of the momentous breadfruit-tree expedition of 1788 he is also a competent connoisseur of the Pacific:

'You will have asked yourself what could have caused the mutiny on the *Bounty*! I can only reply with the assumption that the mutineers could tell that their lives would be better if they stayed on the islands rather than returning to England. That and some of the relationships that were formed with the native women are in my opinion the main causes of those unfortunate events. The leaders of the island were very fond of our people and promised them considerable amounts of property on the island. Subsequently it seems no surprise that some of the seamen were tempted into settling down on the most beautiful island in the world.'

There is a moment of silence between the three men who sit with wistful smiles, immersed in memories of this distant, beloved beauty. Then Bougainville lifts his glass with a sigh that is half regretful and half ironic and proclaims: 'Messieurs, a toast to our noble savages! You fortunate and wise people! I will always remember the moments I spent among you joyfully and for as long as I live, I will praise the wonderful island of La Nouvelle Cythère; she is the true Utopia.'

They drink. After a pause, Forster continues thoughtfully: 'One should sincerely hope that interaction between the Europeans and the South Sea islanders is ended before the depraved customs of the civilised nations infect these innocent people who live so happily in their ignorance and simplicity. But,' he continues with a sigh, 'it is the sad truth that human kindness and European political systems can't co-exist in harmony.'

If it is still unclear, the group of experts were gushing about Tahiti, the new Island of Aphrodite, the centre and epitome of all Pacific transfiguration. Although it is fictional, the dialogue could certainly have taken place, since the comments made by the explorers are quoted from their accounts of their travels.

During the second half of the 18th century they were among the first Europeans to set foot on this mythical and auspicious island. And much more: they helped shape it. Although there had already been some European adventurers, merchants, explorers and pirates who dared to venture into the farther reaches of the Pacific since the 16th century, the first systematic explorations of the oceanic island world took place in the 18th century. The resulting publications of travel documents by Wallis, Cook, Forster, Bougainville and Lapérouse established the myth of the South Seas that still lingers with us today.

The vivid, lyrical, colour-saturated images of an arcadia beneath the tropical sun, so beautiful that it enraptured even such pragmatic characters as Cook and Bligh, caused an uncritically sentimental longing for the South Seas in Europe. Notions of noble savages and a paradise on earth dominated the salons of those days and manifested themselves in philosophy, painting and poetry that are still present today – even if only in the perfect palm-tree beach locations of rum and cigarette advertisements, the aloha whining of Hawaiian guitars or cartoons of deserted tropical islands.

Back during the eve of the Revolution, educated, secular Europe shared a Dionysian dream; the dream of Tahiti. A dream that spread like an epidemic and was as addictive as a drug. Cultural criticism and the tedium of civilisation, pastoral idylls and the longing for the gardens of childhood – all these things could be nicely wrapped in the charmingly printed fabrics, fragrant flower wreaths and shining seashell necklaces from Otaheiti. So there really did exist a counterbalance to the ever more complicated, convoluted reality of war and crisis-ridden Europe: a straightforward and simple world in which untainted humans could live a life of pastoral happiness at one with nature ...

Et in arcadia ego ... No one who read and wrote was spared from South Sea enthusiasm. Rousseau, Diderot, Kant, Wieland, Schiller, Lichtenberg, Chamisso – and countless others let themselves get carried away by the already poetically varnished reports of the explorers to embellish the Tahitian utopia further; far beyond most factual content. The escapist reveries of island life in the blissful primitive state of humanity even went as far as to develop plans of a German colony for poets (Klopstock, Voß, Claudius).

Even old Goethe, who would have greedily devoured anything that was published on the European book market about the newest discoveries in the Pacific, dictated the following querulously longing and yet clear-sightedly modern passage to Eckermann:

'Us old Europeans are all doing more or less badly; our condition is far too artificial and complicated, our nutrition and lifestyle without the right nature, and our social interaction is without real love and goodwill. One should often wish to have been born as a so-called savage on one of the South Sea Islands, just be able to enjoy pure human existence without a bad aftertaste. If in a depressed mood and thinking ones way deeply into the misery of our times, it almost seems as though the world were slowly readying itself for the Last Judgement.'

Under the influence of Rousseau, the discoverers and correspondents saw what they wanted to see and overlooked – or couldn't see – those things that didn't correspond to their ideals. Of course the Polynesian world was not a paradise on earth; the Tahitians also lived in man-made communities bound by a strict and complicated social and political system that gave each person a specific place limited by clear boundaries. Breaking free – whereto remains the question – was not possible. There was a rigid social pyramid of sovereigns, priests, free people and slaves,

there was a religion that claimed its rights unyield-
ingly, there were human sacrifices and infanticide,
and there was war.

Yet before white people began to exercise their
influence, this social structure really did give individuals living within its balanced boundaries the opportunity of 'enjoying human existence in its pure form'.
It was not only the philanthropist Georg Forster who
in the early meeting stages predicted that the encounter between the oceanic peoples and the whites would
define the future. Particularly once the Pacific was
divided into spheres of political influence and colonial exploitation could take place.

Before that, Bougainville stated openly what the
conquest of the Pacific was really all about: 'All the
riches of the earth belong to Europe, who has made sci-
ences the sovereign of the rest of the world. Let us go
and bring in the harvest! The South Sea will become
an inexhaustible source for the export of French prod-
ucts that will be used by the countless peoples who
live there and who, in the state of ignorance in which
they live, will accept them indefinitely.'

One couldn't have put it more clearly. It seems obvious that the last thing he thought of in his appeal to entrepreneurial daringness was that the first export goods with the most long-term effects were called: sickness, death and suffering. Measles, influenza, tuberculosis, smallpox, typhoid, whooping cough and countless other Western diseases that were unknown on the islands and therefore could not be resisted by the islanders' immune systems, decimated entire archipelagos in the following decades and even continued to do so until the beginning of the 20th century. Alcohol and venereal diseases did the rest. (Cook and Bougainville even fought a macabre feud over whose crew was responsible for the spread of syphilis on Tahiti.)

After the explorers the missionaries arrived. Then came the merchants, garrisons and colonial officials. These were followed by planters, sandalwood cutters, trepang fishermen and whalers. Then came the phosphate miners, art thieves, ethnologists, development workers and atom bomb testers. Then came the adventurers, the banished, the stranded, the beachcombers and finally tourists from all over the world.

Western civilisation descended upon the islands. It destroyed existing structures, crushed ancient cultures, arbitrarily mixed nationalities and levelled out regional autonomies.

But in spite of everything the myth of paradise on earth, of simple contented life on the islands in the light, turned out to be resilient over time. Its most famous victim and simultaneously its most famous culprit: the painter Paul Gauguin. When he decided to turn his back on Western civilisation and dare to start a radically new life on Tahiti he wrote (and you should believe his words): 'The natives, the fortunate inhabitants of this unknown oceanic paradise live only for the pleasures and delights of existence.' But only a few days after his arrival on Tahiti in 1891 the absconder noted with disillusion: 'But this was Europe – the Europe from which I had believed to have released myself – and that under the aggravating aspect of colonial snobbism and a childish, bordering on caricature-like, grotesque imitation.'

And yet Gauguin's mysteriously glowing paintings from Tahiti and Hiva Oa remain particularly impressive for their intrinsic representation of the South Sea myth that has been carried forth to the present day.

In 1913, only ten days after Gauguin's death, Emil Nolde, who had also moved away to find a paradise far removed from the rest of the world, wrote a résumé of his travels in the South Pacific islands which rings true nowadays more so than ever: 'If the coloured natives should ever write a colonial history from their perspective, then the Europeans will have to crawl into caves in shame. One thing is certain: We, the white Europeans are the misfortune of the coloured primitive peoples – and the Japanese are diligently following suit. America has already done its part.'

Tropique

Canton
I. Formosa

GRAND

INDE

I. Hai-nan

MER DE LA CHINE

Manilla

PHILIPPINES

I. Palaouan

I. Mindanao

I. Soulou

Borneo

ARCHIPEL INDIEN

OCÉAN

Iles Carolines

Gouaham

I.ᵉˢ Mariannes

Tinian

Palaos ou I. Peleu

Yap

Ligne

MER

G.ᵉ de Siam

Dét. de Malacca

Malacca

M.ᵗ Ophyr

Padang

M.ᵗ Indrapoura

Bencoulen

Palembang

Banca

Billiton

Pt. de Macassar

CÉLÈBES

Ternate

MOLUQUES

I. Gilolo

I. Céram

Banda

I.ᵈᵉ l'Amirauté

NOUVELLE GUINÉE

N.ˡˡᵉ Irlande

N.ˡˡᵉ Bretagne

Bougainville

Louisiade

Batavia

JAVA

Macassar

Sambao

Petites Iles Flores

Timor

Teuimber I.

ILES DE LA SONDE

Dét. de la SONDE

MER DES

Tropique

B. du Geograph.

INDES

ou

OCÉAN

INDIEN

R. Murchison

Fremantle & R. des Cygnes

C. Leuwin

Albany et P.ᵗ du Roi Georges

Terre de Witt

NOUVELLE HOLLANDE

Terre d'Endracht

I. Melville

I. Bathurst

Pt. Essington

Port Darwin

D. de Carpentarie

D. de Torres

C. York

C. Somerset

Cooktown

Herberton

Denison

Rockhampton

North Australia

M.ᵗ Central

L. Amadeus

M.ᵗ Olga

Western Australia

AUSTRALIE

dont l'étendue est évaluée aux ⅘ de celle de l'Europe

L. Eyre

South Australia

Adelaide

Murray

VICTORIA

Melbourne

D. de Bass

Maryborough

Gympie

Brisbane

Warwick

NOUVELLE GALLES DU SUD

New South Wales

Sidney et

Pt. Wilson

T. de Diemen ou Tasmanie

Hobart-town

OCÉANIE